Political and Social Economy Series
Edited by C. Addison Hickman and Michael P. Shields

Other Books in This Series:

CONGLOMERATES
and the
Evolution of Capitalism

By Charles R. Spruill

SOUTHERN ILLINOIS UNIVERSITY PRESS

Carbondale and Edwardsville

Printed in the United States of America
Edited by D. Vincent Varallo
Designed by Bob Nance, Design for Publishing
Second printing May 1983

Library of Congress Cataloging in Publication Data

Spruill, Charles R.
    Conglomerates and the evolution of capitalism.

    (Political and social economy series)
    Bibliography: p. 172
    Includes index.
    1. Conglomerate Corporations--United States.
2. Diversification in industry--United States.
3. United States--Economic conditions--1971-1981.
4. Capitalism.   I. Title.   II. Series.
HD2756.2.U5S67   338.8'042   81-4458
ISBN 0-8093-1012-0   AACR2

In Memoriam

ARTHUR M. FORD
Scholar, Teacher, and Friend

Contents

Tables

Figures

Acknowledgments

THIS BOOK was written while I was a faculty member of Hobart and William Colleges. I am deeply grateful to this institution as it provided me with a research grant, a sabbatical leave, and all the supportive services necessary to make this book possible. I was especially fortunate to have three excellent secretaries, Valerie O'Malley, Pat Zrebiec, and Carla Tobia; a most conscientious research assistant, Lorie Dixon; a helpful colleague in the computer science department, Dick Albright; a very capable librarian, Gary Thompson. Vincent Varallo, editorial assistant, Southern Illinois University Press, demonstrated great expertise and patience in guiding this work to publication.

Earlier drafts of the entire manuscript were read by Milton T. Edelman, C. Addison Hickman, Michael Shields, while Henry Steele read an earlier draft of chapter 3. Several very insightful comments were received through correspondence with Walter Adams and Robert Conn. Tony Broh was most helpful regarding the discussion of political action committees in chapter 5 and in collecting the data that are included in the appendixes to that chapter. The most support I received, both personally and professionally, came from my wife, Pat, who read every page of every draft. Her help was invaluable.

Of course, any failings, mistakes, omissions or misconceptions are entirely my own and do not reflect the judgment or values of those mentioned above.

Spring, 1981   Charles R. Spruill
Boone, North Carolina

1 Introduction

THE SUBJECT of this book is the emergence of large, diversified enterprises in the American national economy. The larger and more diversified of these firms have been labeled conglomerates. Conglomerates are firms which face numerous distinct markets, each with its own supply, demand, and profit characteristics. Large, diversified firms are not entirely new to the economy. They have existed to some extent for many years. But, since World War II there has been an increase in their numbers and their degree of diversification.

The purpose of this book is to analyze the dynamics of firm diversification and to answer the following questions: Why would a firm want to diversify? How have labor unions responded to the increased presence of diversified firms? What influence does the effort of many, large firms diversifying exert on the evolution of capitalism? What policy implications can be derived from this kind of economic activity? Hypotheses regarding conglomerate enterprises, as often as not, are shrouded in conjecture because these firms do not fit nicely into any of the structural theories that are standard today. They are not trying to monopolize one market, or act as an oligopolist in one market. They are active in many markets. We want to find answers to the questions posed above so that we can help reduce the speculation surrounding conglomerates today.

A discussion of present day conglomerate firms requires some familiarity with their corporate predecessor, the holding company of the late nineteenth and early twentieth centuries. It has been

always true that states have held the power of incorporation. Prior to 1888, states rarely allowed
a firm to incorporate if the firm proposed to own
other corporations or produce more than one product. Then in 1888, New Jersey, in search of a tax
base for its economy, passed a law that allowed
incorporation of firms which proposed to acquire
other firms and/or several product lines.[1] The
passage of this law cleared the way for the birth
of firms known as holding companies. A holding
company is a company which either exercises control or has the ability to exercise control over
one or more other companies. Prior to 1888, only a
few corporations could be considered holding companies and these were typically public utilities
which had exemptions from the state laws. With the
passage of the New Jersey Law, other states quickly
responded by passing similar laws so that New Jersey would not gain a monopoly on corporate charters and hence on corporate business and taxes.
The classic question asked at the time was: What
is the purpose of a holding company? (The same
question is being asked today regarding conglomerates.) Adolf Berle and Gardiner Means made the
argument that the holding company facilitated an
easy avenue to increased control, by a few managements, over the physical assets of the economy.[2]

An example of a technique used to facilitate
this control is pyramiding. Pyramiding refers to a
situation in which one corporation owns a majority
of the stock of another corporation which, in
turn, holds a majority of the stock of yet a third
corporation, and so forth. It is easy to see that,
through pyramiding, a holding company could even
own other holding companies. The importance of
this is that to control a huge amount, only a
small amount is required. For example, suppose
Company XYZ has $30 million in debt and equity
outstanding. Assume that this is composed of $10
million each in bonds, preferred nonvoting stock,
and common stock. The control of Company XYZ can
be achieved through the ownership of approximately
$5 million of common stock. A group of investors
could purchase $5 million in common stock and gain
voting control. With a holding company, though,
$5 million is not necessary. The group can sell
the $5 million common of XYZ to a holding company
which they create. The holding company exchanges
$1 million of its own bonds, $2 million in pre-

ferred stock (nonvoting), and $2 million of common
stock. The group can then sell off the bonds, preferred stock, and $1 million of the common. Thus,
with $1 million common it controls the holding
company which, in turn, controls $5 million of
Company XYZ, worth $30 million. Repeating this
procedure, a second holding company could be
created to buy half of the common stock of the
first company. This type of arrangement was typical in the 1920s. In fact, John K. Galbraith, com-
menting on the demise of the stock market and the
onset of the Great Depression, noted that the
holding companies, characterized by a great degree
of pyramiding, were largely responsible.[3] As the
stock market faltered, these companies had great
difficulty raising funds to meet cash flow obligations. This exacerbated the already shaky confidence of investors. Due to this pyramid of finance,
the holding company was now too weak at its base
to meet the financial comments it had acquired.
Many firms went bankrupt and Galbraith referred to
this as "devastation by reverse leverage."[4] He
further noted that "nothing of equal extravagence
has yet appeared to take their (holding companies)
place."[5] It has become the contention of several
contemporary economists that the conglomerate
surge, which began after World War II and which
continues today, may well represent a phenomenon
of equal extravagence.[6]

Firm diversification occurs one of two ways. A
firm may move into a new market de novo, that is,
through internal growth, or through acquisition of
an existing firm. Acquisitions are generally considered more popular since they are quicker and
involve less uncertainty. It is possible to esti-
mate the degree of conglomerate activity in the
economy by noting the number of conglomerate type
mergers that have taken place in recent years as
shown in Table 1.1.

The Federal Trade Commission (FTC) separates
conglomerate mergers into three categories. Product extension mergers refer to mergers between
two firms with related but not identical products;
market extension refers to mergers between firms
that produce the same product but in a different
geographical market; the category "other" refers
to mergers between firms that produce totally
unrelated products. Table 1.1 indicates that, by
number of mergers or volume of assets, conglomerate

TABLE 1.1

Types of Recent Merger Activity

Acquisition in U.S. Mining and Manufacturing, of over $10 Million Asset Value

| | By Number of Mergers | | | | By Volume of Mergers | | | |
| | Number | | Percentage | | Assets ($billion) | | Percentage | |
	1948–1964	1965–1976	1948–1964	1965–1976	1948–1964	1965–1975	1948–1964	1965–1975
Horizontal	147	129	23	12	4,969	8,818	22	13
Vertical	94	85	14	8	3,974	3,748	19	6
Conglomerate	406	846	63	80	12,578	54,455	59	81
Product-Extension	270	481	42	45	8,076	22,714	38	34
Market-Extension	35	41	5	4	1,064	5,315	5	8
Other	101	324	16	31	3,437	26,426	16	39
Total	647	1,060	100	100	21,521	67,020	100	100

SOURCE: Federal Trade Commission, Bureau of Economics, Statistical Report on Mergers and Acquisitions, November, 1977 (Washington, D.C.: U.S. Government Printing Office, 1977).

mergers accounted for about 60% of the total number of mergers in the period 1948-1964 and about
80% of those in 1965-1975.

Conglomerate mergers did not always dominate
the merger scene. In earlier periods, horizontal
mergers (mergers between firms producing the same
product) and vertical mergers (mergers between
firms in different steps of the production process) were more popular. The great trusts grew out
of horizontal and vertical mergers that took place
in two merger waves, one in 1895-1904 and the
other in 1920-1930.[7] One of the most famous trusts
was Standard Oil of New Jersey. In 1870, Standard
Oil of New Jersey was incorporated and, during the
next two decades, it captured 90% of the petroleum
refining industry through merger.[8] The railroad
industry, very crucial in this historic period of
expansion, was also subject to merger and takeover.
Morgan, Vanderbilt, Carnegie, Hillard, Hill, Gould,
and Harriman, all railroad barons, were continuously attempting to monopolize the industry, sometimes through collusion, other times through cut-
throat competition.[9] As the dominant firms in
these industries became entrenched and their monopoly prices set, the public objected to these
trusts and demanded government intervention. This
culminated in the passage of the Sherman Antitrust
Act of 1890. Section 2 of this Act states in part:
"Every person who shall monopolize, or attempt to
monopolize, or combine or conspire with any other
person or persons to monopolize any part of the
trade or commerce . . . shall be guilty of a mis-
demeanor."[10]

Shortly after the passage of the Sherman Act,
the federal government prosecuted the Northern
Securities Company, a holding company that controlled two competing railroad lines, The Great
Northern and The Northern Pacific. The Supreme
Court, in 1904, ordered the dissolution of the
Northern Securities Company.[11] In 1911, the Court
found Standard Oil of New Jersey guilty of unrea-
sonable restraint of trade and dissolution was
ordered. This decision by the Court to find Standard Oil guilty under the Sherman Act established
the Act as a viable means of dealing with monopoly
in the marketplace. A severe price was paid,
though, since the Court interjected the concept of
the "rule of reason" into the case and this ultimately weakened the statute. According to Chief

Justice White, a strict interpretation of Section 2 was incorrect. That is, "It is not merely the fact of a contract, combination of conspiracy in restraint of trade that is at issue . . . but also the nature of the restraint . . . and rule of reason becomes the guide."[12]

The merger wave of 1895-1904 brought pressure on Congress to further reduce the opportunity for firms to monopolize particular markets. The preeminant merger of all time, involving the creation of U.S. Steel, took place during this era. In 1890, the steel industry had a competitive structure; between 1890 and 1900 most of the steel firms merged into about twenty enterprises. In 1901, J. P. Morgan, with the support of Carnegie, combined twelve of these twenty enterprises into one, U.S. Steel. What began as 170 firms in 1890, became one by 1901.[13] Shortly thereafter, the government charged U.S. Steel with monopoly and attempting to monopolize the steel industry under Section 2 of the Sherman Act.

In 1920, U.S. Steel was judged not guilty of violating the Sherman Act because, even though it had attempted to monopolize the steel industry, it had failed. The failure had occurred, in part, because the tactics it had used were not as repugnant as those which had been used by Standard Oil. The fact that it had failed in its attempt to monopolize the steel industry, together with the fact that it had used civil tactics, led the Court to rule that U.S. Steel was a reasonable trust. This case set the stage for a weakening of the Sherman Act.

Even before the U.S. Steel case was decided, Congress realized that the 1911 Standard Oil of New Jersey decision which implemented the "rule of reason" had substantially weakened the Sherman Act. Therefore, in 1914, it passed the Clayton Act to shore up the intent of the Sherman Act. Of the five sections directed at antitrust violators, Section 7 is particularly relevant. It "prohibits corporations from holding the stock of another company or of two competing companies where the effect . . . may be to substantially lessen competition.[14]

Unfortunately for the framers of the Clayton Act, corporations proceeded to obtain ownership by buying the assets of other corporations instead of buying stock. Thus Section 7 did not prevent hold-

ing companies from striving to achieve their goal
of obtaining control over the assets of the economy. Congress did not react immediately to this
end run tactic.

In 1948, after hearing the Columbia Steel case,
the Supreme Court ruled that it was legal for U.S.
Steel (the largest manufacturer of steel at that
time) to purchase the assets of Consolidated Steel,
a major steel fabricator. The implication was that
if Congress did not want this type of merger to
take place, it would have to pass legislation
explicitly prohibiting it.

In 1950, Congress responded by passing the
Celler-Kefauver amendment to Section 7 of the
Clayton Act. It stated

> That no corporation engaged in commerce shall
> acquire, directly or indirectly, the whole or
> any part of the stock or other share capital
> and no corporation subject to the jurisdic-
> tion of the Federal Trade Commission shall
> acquire the whole or any part of the assets
> of another corporation engaged also in com-
> merce, where in any line of commerce in any
> section of the country, the effect of such
> acquisition may be substantially to lessen
> competition, or to tend to create a mono-
> poly.[15]

The passage of this amendment substantially increased the difficulty associated with firms
acquiring other firms. This pertains to mergers
that are either horizontal or vertical in nature.
The Courts, since 1950, have held that "horizontal
mergers in which one or both firms are market
leaders violate Section 7; and vertical mergers
that involve significant foreclosure are similarly
condemned."[16]

Some economists believe that, as a result of
this legislation, corporations interested in growth
have been given the incentive to become multi-
product firms. That is, in their attempts to
acquire assets, firms have found the least resis-
tance when they branch out into new markets. Data
presented in Table 1.1 lend support that there was
a significant decline in the percent of horizontal
and vertical mergers after the passage of the
Celler-Kefauver amendment in 1950, and a considerable increase in the number of conglomerate mer-

gers. Irwin Stelzer, in testifying before the
Senate Subcommittee on Antitrust and Monopoly,
observed that "the first reason given (for diversification) is government policy; that is, the rigid
enforcement of the Clayton Act, has inadvertantly
supported diversification activity."[17] Stelzer
also testified that "the trend toward conglomerate
acquisition has produced more diversified companies
and has undoubtedly kept concentration levels in
specific industries below those that would have
been obtained otherwise."[18]

The positive result that industry concentration
levels have been kept at moderating levels due to
antitrust laws may have some negative aspects. A
reduction in market power (the degree of dominance
by any one firm over a particular market) may
cause a net increase in economic power (the degree
of control by any firm or group of firms over the
resources of the economy). It is feasible that
moderating concentration ratios in each of a set
of industries may actually cause increasing aggregate concentration. This argument has been made by
the FTC for quite some time. Also, Willard Mueller
noted that the two hundred largest manufacturing
firms have used the merger device to "yield them a
grossly disproportionate share of the top four
positions in precisely those industries that are
highly concentrated."[19] He studied 135 manufacturing industries in 1963 and found that the two hundred largest manufacturing firms accounted for
"63% to 87% of the value added to those . . .
industries where the four firm concentration ratio
was 51% to 100% versus a modest 14% to 31% share
of the value added in those . . . industries with
a 4 firm concentration ratio of less than 50%."[20]
Mueller concluded: "In short, this handful of
giant firms has used the corporate merger device
to capture the high ground of the American economy,
the commanding market shares in the highly concentrated, highly differentiated oligopolies where
the largest profits are regularly earned."[21]

Aggregate concentration has been rising steadily but not rapidly since the beginning of the
twentieth century.[22] This rise, resulting partly
from firm diversification, suggests a need for a
better understanding of diversified growth. The
structure of the economy is taking on a different
look, namely, one that is made up of large, multi-
product firms which operate in many markets. What

needs to be identified is the absolute and relative size of the largest manufacturing firms and
the degree of control they have over the assets of
the manufacturing sector of the economy. A question posed by Charles Berry is central to our discussion:

> Market structure, however, is not the same
> thing as the corporate structure of indus-
> try . . . The size of a particular firm--
> in toto, counting all its sales or assets--
> is irrelevant to the determination of the
> relative contribution of its sales within
> a particular market. The corporate struc-
> ture of industry--measures of the relative
> size of firms--can change quite indepen-
> dently of the structure of markets . . .
> The interesting question is what consider-
> ation of corporate size adds to the signif-
> icance of market structure in the analysis
> of industry performance.[23]

Over the last decade, the largest manufacturing
corporations have controlled most of the assets in
that sector. In 1968, the 1,000 largest firms held
80.8% of the total manufacturing assets in the
economy; of this 80.8%, the 200 largest manufacturing firms held 75.6%, or 61.1% of the total
manufacturing assets in the economy.[24] In 1978,
the 200 largest manufacturing firms held 76.4% of
the assets of the 1,000 largest manufacturing
firms.[25] If one considers the actual size of these
firms, the disparity in economic power is apparent.
Looking at Table 1.2, the largest firm by asset
size, Exxon, had $38,453,336,000 in assets. The
ten largest firms range from $38,453,336,000 to
$12,884,286,000. The two hundredth largest firm
had assets of $934,180,000 and the one hundredth
largest $1,844,034,000.[26] The rapid decline in
size is quite evident here.
Figures 1.1 and 1.2 show Lorenz Curves for the
years 1968 and 1978 respectively. A Lorenz Curve
illustrates the degree of inequality in asset size.
The diagonal line represents a perfectly equal
distribution of assets among the largest 1,000
firms. The further the data points are from the
diagonal line, the less equal is the distribution
of assets. The degree of inequality can be measures by a Gini coefficient.[27] In 1968 the Gini

TABLE 1.2

The 10 Largest Industrial Corporations
by Assets, 1977

Company	Assets ($billion)	Rank
Exxon (New York)	$38,453,336	1
General Motors (Detroit)	26,658,300	2
Mobil (New York)	20,575,967	3
Ford Motor (Dearborn, Mich.)	19,241,300	4
IBM (Armonk, N. Y.)	18,978,445	5
Texaco (White Plains, N. Y.)	18,926,026	6
Standard Oil of California (San Francisco)	14,822,347	7
Gulf Oil (Pittsburgh)	14,225,000	8
General Electric (Fairfield, Conn.)	13,696,800	9
Standard Oil (Ind.)	12,884,286	10

coefficient for the above data was 0.67, tending
to be closer to one and hence toward an unequal
distribution.[28] In 1977 the Gini coefficient was
0.63, again indicating a rather unequal distribution.[29] What this analysis demonstrates is that
the largest manufacturing firms are large both
relatively and absolutely.

When one adds the dimension of diversification
to size, the concept of power is expanded. As
stated earlier, one definition of power refers to
market (monopoly) power and measures the degree
of dominance of a firm over a particular industry.
The larger a firm's market share, the greater its
ability to set price at will, hence, the greater
its market power. Economic power, on the other
hand, refers to a measure of a firm's control over
assets (resources) in the economy (or in a sector
of the economy). A firm is said to be economically
powerful if it is "large" in size; that is if it
controls a disproportionate amount of the assets
of an economy (or a sector of the economy). Another
form of power is diversification power, which refers to the ability of a firm to shift resources
among the markets in which it is involved and
thereby reduce its dependence on any one market
for survival.[30] Finally, there is conglomerate
power. It exists when a firm is large, diversified,
and has market power in some, if not all, of the

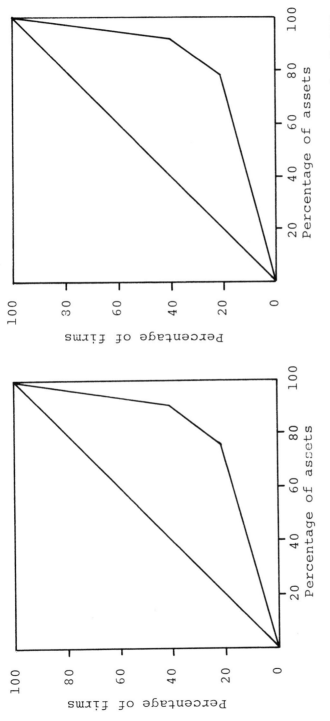

Fig. 1.1. Lorenz Curve of the 1,000 largest industrial firms, 1968

SOURCE: Hearings before the Senate Sub-committee on Antitrust and Monopoly, 1969, overall and conglomerate aspects, pt. 8A, App. A, pp. 704-705.

Fig. 1.2. Lorenz Curve of the 1,000 largest industrial firms, 1977

SOURCE: Fortune Magazine, May and June issues, 1978.

markets in which it operates. As Corwin Edwards has stated:

> It (conglomerate power) is derived from two facts: first, that the enterprise has re-sources much larger than those of most of its competitors; and second, that these re-sources are spread across many markets. . . .
> Money is power, a big firm can outbid, out-spend and outlose a small firm. It can ad-vertise more intensively . . . buy up in-ventions of others, defend its legal rights . . . more thoroughly, bid higher for scarce resources, acquire the best locations and the best technicians and executives.[31]

An example of conglomerate power is evident in the case of A&P and the Philadelphia grocery store market. In the early 1960s, A&P--the nation's largest chain--operated in 1,000 different commu-nities. In the Philadelphia market, A&P stood well down the ladder in terms of market share. This fact not withstanding, "it was concluded that A&P was the price leader in the area, not because of its position in Philadelphia, where it was not the largest chain, but because of its national strength. . . . A&P's nationwide strength was repeatedly cited as a factor explaining its abil-ity to serve as price leader."[32] The dominant firms in the market allowed A&P to be the price leader because of its conglomerate power. The leading firms in this particular market avoided the serious consequences that could have resulted if they had tried to press their prices on A&P. A&P could outspend, outbid, and outlose any one or any group of those firms.

2 Motives for Diversification

JUDGING from the recent, sharp increase in the
number of conglomerate mergers in the economy, it
would appear that firms have a great incentive to
diversify. One explanation of why firms become
conglomerates is that economies of scale may be
realized. Economies of scale refer to the reduction in average cost realized by the firm as output increases. Alternatively, diseconomies of
scale refer to increases in average cost as output increases. There are many costs that are
embodied in a total cost function, and each plays
a role in determining the shape of the total cost
curve. Technical economies refer to average cost
reductions that are realized in the actual physical process of combining inputs to produce output.
Pecuniary economies refer to savings in the areas
of purchasing and finance, while nonpecuniary
economies refer to savings in advertising and
sales promotion. Total cost, then, equals technical costs plus pecuniary costs plus nonpecuniary
costs. Average total cost (ATC) is derived from
total cost and therefore is influenced by these
same variables. ATC curves have several forms.
They may be U shaped and have either a steep gradient, a gentle gradient, or an extended minimum
cost range. The downward sloping part of the ATC
curve is caused by the economies experienced over
the lower levels of production while, at higher
levels, diseconomies cause the ATC curve to slope
upward.

It is also possible for the ATC curve to be
flat throughout and thereby exhibit constant
return to scale. If this is the case, the firm

experiences neither economies nor diseconomies of
scale as it increases production. Even though all
firms do not tend to exhibit identically shaped
ATC curves, most firms do experience some economies of scale in early stages of production and
some diseconomies later at higher levels of output.
The gradients vary, but most firms face some type
of U shaped curve.[1]

If one extends the discussion of cost to a
multi-plant firm, producing a single product, the
analysis changes somewhat. A multi-plant firm will
face a set of ATC curves, one for each plant. If
having several plants causes neither economies nor
diseconomies to the firm overall, then the relevant envelope curve will be horizontal. Here, a
proportional increase in output (say the addition
of a new plant producing at minimum cost) would
yield no increase in ATC. It is possible that having a multi-plant operation could reduce ATC
through certain economies, in which case the cost
curve would fall as output rises. In contrast, diseconomies could be experienced due to a multi-
plant operation causing costs to rise as output
rises. These concepts can be applied to the conglomerate firm.

It is not easy to separate empirically the
three components of total cost when trying to
identify the impact each has on the shape of a
firm's ATC curve.[2] However, an analytical separa-
tion is fairly easy to accomplish. Technical economies accrue due to the degree of capital required,
the degree of specialization and division of labor
achieved, and the physical laws and laws of multi-
ples engaged; pecuniary economies may be realized
due to savings in procuring inputs and in financial accounting; nonpecuniary economies could be
experienced in promotion and advertising.[3]

A conglomerate, by producing in unrelated markets, could face a spectrum of unique production
functions. Therefore, as the firm diversifies, it
should not expect to realize technical economies
of scale.[4] It is possible, however, that both
pecuniary and nonpecuniary economies may be experienced. John Narver has noted that

> A significant commonality of inputs clearly
> can enhance economies in purchasing raw ma-
> terials. With manufacturing or processing
> commonalities, economies accrue through

intrafirm joint use of plant and equipment,
and utilization of by-products, scrap, and
managerial knowledge. Savings in insurance
and in shared administrative research and
technical services are often feasible.[5]

Thus, the conglomerate may be able to economize on
management services by sharing a common pool of
accountants, financial planners, market research-
ers, labor relations experts, lawyers, and/or purchasing agents.[6] In addition, the conglomerate may
be able to manipulate demand and supply within the
firm so that certain subsidiaries may be able to
purchase inputs from one another thereby reducing
excess capacity for the firm as a whole. We will
return to this point in our discussion of reciprocity.
    There is the possibility that large firms may
wrest price concession from smaller firms. This
practice results in what is called pecuniary economies in procurement. Also, large, diversified
firms have a cost advantage as they attempt to
raise financial resources. Because financial institutions consider these firms to be the best
customers, they are given the lowest possible
rates of interest on loans, and they are also considered first for the available loanable funds. Of
course, the greater the amount of the loan, the
lower is the per-dollar-transactions cost; therefore, the smaller firms, which typically do not
require as much capital as the large conglomerates,
pay a higher cost per dollar of capital borrowed.
    Nonpecuniary economies could influence costs
since economies of scale exist in the area of advertising and sales promotion. Joe S. Bain, in
discussing sales of consumer goods concluded that
product differentiation was

> of at least the same general order of impor-
> tance . . . as economies of large scale pro-
> duction and distribution in giving estab-
> lished market leaders a price or cost advan-
> tage over rivals. Moreover, when industry
> leaders possessed especially large price or
> cost advantages over small rivals or poten-
> tial industry entrants, it was typically
> because of successful product differentia-
> tion rather than production or distribution
> scale economies.[7]

Large firms have an advantage because they can
afford to advertise more and on a larger scale.
In newspapers and magazines, full-page ads are
less expensive per square inch than small ads.
Also, ads placed nationally are cheaper per reader
than those placed regionally.[8]

In the case of television advertising, not only
do the large firms have resources to purchase huge
blocks of time, but their requests to buy time
often take precedence over the smaller firms. For
instance, Blair found that smaller firms could not
get sixty-second prime time television spots; all
had been taken by the large firms. In addition,
when a small firm was fortunate enough to be able
to purchase a twenty-second commercial, the cost
was not one-third of a sixty-second commercial but
90%.[9] A good source of evidence of economies of
scale in advertising can be found in the Proctor
and Gamble-Clorox merger case.

> In the year before merger Clorox had obtained
> 592,000 seconds of television time, and after
> merger with Proctor and Gamble, 803,060 sec-
> onds of television time with no change in
> advertising expenditures. This represented
> an increase of 35.6 percent and fully justi-
> fied the Commission's (FTC) finding that at
> least 33 1/3 percent more network television
> advertising could be obtained for the same
> amount of money when Clorox became part of
> the Proctor line.[10]

Obviously those conglomerate firms producing consumer goods would be affected by this to a greater
extent than those which do not since advertising
generally is used more heavily in consumer-goods
industries.

Within reasonable limits, any group of diverse
firms in the economy face the same kinds of technological and institutional constraints. They have
to operate within the confines of our technological know-how, deal with the same set of sociolog-
ical mores, the same financial and accounting pro-
cedures, and the same promotional agencies. While
economies of scale may not be realized by conglomerates in the technical production processes,
there are many possibilities for economies in the
pecuniary and nonpecuniary areas. Largeness
enhances a firm's opportunity to borrow loanable

funds and to get more advertising time and space
for less funds.

Just as there are possible economies of scale
that may be experienced due to diversification,
there may be diseconomies as well. These diseconomies
stem mainly from the organizational difficulties
that arise with large size. There has to be
an increase in the size of the staff responsible
for disseminating information between the various
subsidiaries of the firm, and even if there is a
somewhat decentralized decision-making process in
a conglomerate, there is still a need for overall
coordination. The conglomerate nature of the firm
may cause diseconomies due to the increased burden
of overhead charges. While economies may result
from the pooling of services, there may be an increase
in the number of services needed to keep a
diversified firm operating. Intersubsidiary committees
may be necessary to keep the conglomerate
abreast of the various activities of the subparts.
While costs of outside services may go down, costs
for internal services may go up.

Regarding economies of scale and firm diversification,
multi-product firms, like other types of
firms, also face the possibilities of their envelope-cost
curve rising, remaining constant, or
declining as output increases (product lines
added). As we have noted, with diversification the
firm should not expect to experience any technical
economies or diseconomies of scale. Thus, with an
increase in output due to an added product line,
the conglomerate would be expected to realize constant
average total costs if technical economies
were the only type of cost. However, this is not
the case. There are pecuniary economies that may
accrue as well as nonpecuniary. For conglomerates,
if these were realized, the result would be a declining
cost curve, ceteris paribus, as more product
lines were acquired.

There are diseconomies that may occur as well.
If this was the case, ceteris paribus, the envelope
curve would rise as new product lines were
added. As a conglomerate continues to diversify,
it probably experiences both economies and diseconomies
of scale. The particulars related to the
product lines accumulated would determine the
weights of the economies relative to the diseconomies.
If the conglomerate were to become quite
large, then pecuniary economies could be a major

factor as the firm experienced savings in purchasing, finance, and overhead expenditures. If a considerable number of the lines offered were consumer products, then nonpecuniary economies in advertising could become the major factor in determining the gradient of the envelope curve. However, after some degree of expansion, largeness per se could become the major factor and diseconomies of scale could outweigh any and all economies. At this point the envelope cost curve would begin to rise. The only information not known to the conglomerate before the fact is beyond what point of diversification will diseconomies begin to outweigh previously experienced economies. Since conglomerates should not expect to realize technical economies, motives for diversification must rest on pecuniary and nonpecuniary economies. However, the diseconomies that are almost inevitable after some level of activity should become a discouraging factor for continued diversification.

The concept of X-inefficiency refers to the inefficient use of resources in the production process. The discussion of costs in the previous paragraphs assumed that the cost curves represented the set of points of minimum cost for given levels of output. The points along the curve in Figure 2.1 represent the absolute minimum levels of cost.

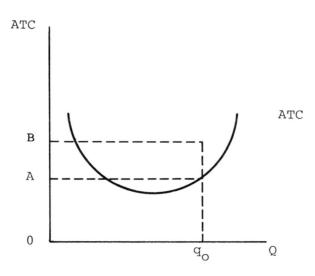

Fig. 2.1. Minimum levels of cost

If there is an inefficient use of resources, this
level of cost will not be attained. For a given
level of output, say q_0, the most efficient method
of production would yield average cost OA while an
inefficient method would yield a higher cost, say
OB. It has been argued by Harvey Leibenstein and
others that X-inefficiency is prevalent in certain
sectors of the economy.[11] Frederic Scherer esti-
mates it at about 10% of the costs of a typical
firm.[12] Leibenstein referred to this inefficiency
when he noted that "firms and economies do not
operate on an outer bound production possibility
surface consistent with their resources. Rather
they actually work on a production surface that is
well within that outer bound. This means that for
a variety of reasons people and organizations nor-
mally neither work as hard nor as effectively as
they could."[13]

The phenomena of X-inefficiency occurs due to a
lack of competitive pressure on the firm. That is,
the existence of imperfect competition in the marketplace is conducive to laxity on the part of
management and leads to "organizational slack."[14]
The firm allows the production process, as well as
the management team, to become too large and un-
wieldy. In addition, the lack of competitive pressure allows the firm to continue with obsolete
production methods and equipment. Thus, the luxury
of a secure, profitable niche in the economy may
lead the managers and workers to substitute variables other than efficiency to be maximized. Such
variables could be grandeur, an easier life style,
and/or the avoidance of risk.[15] If X-inefficiency
does exist in a particular product line, it may be
a signal to conglomerates to seek diversification
along this line.

The reason a conglomerate would consider X-
inefficiency as an incentive for diversification
relates to the corollary to X-inefficiency, namely,
X-efficiency. Here the emphasis is on devising
methods so that more output can be attained from
the same level of inputs.[16] In situations where a
conglomerate firm diversified through acquisition,
the mere presence of a new management structure
within the acquired firm, coupled with the inevitable infusion of new ideas, may be a sufficient
stimulus to increase efficiency and enhance profits.

It has been suggested that modern managerial
techniques have provided an incentive for diversi-

fication. These new techniques include mathematical and statistical analysis and the full use of computers for management and accounting activities (in 1950 only a few computers were in use in business--in 1968 there were over 20,000).[17] Old, established firms which have not taken advantage of these new techniques are, by definition, operating with varied degrees of X-inefficiency. This may lead conglomerates, equipped with more modern techniques, to seek control of such firms.

This line of reasoning would also suggest that firms have the ability to become large conglomerates and simultaneously maintain efficient production methods. New management science and technology afford a management group the opportunity to operate larger, more diversified entities without realizing diseconomies of scale as quickly as would be dictated by antiquated methods. So, the existence of X-inefficiency in one form coupled with another firm's ability to turn X-inefficiency into X-efficiency could be one of the propellants behind the diversification movement currently taking place.

Another possible motive for diversification has to do with corporate earnings and stock market prices. Three distinct theories have evolved regarding earnings, stock prices, and diversification: one, healthy firms seek failing firms; two, failing firms seek healthy firms (the defensive strategy argument); and three, healthy firms seek healthy firms. The term healthy refers to firms experiencing normal to above normal rates of return; the term failing refers to firms experiencing below normal returns or losses.

The first possibility refers to the situation in which a healthy firm will ferret out a failing firm because of the cheap price of its stock, assuming that the stock market is efficient and has reacted to a firm's declining earnings by forcing the price of its stock down. Another firm may consider the lower price to be fair and would thus be enticed to acquire the stock. The reasoning is that the acquiring firm feels that the intrinsic value of the stock is greater than the level merited by the failing firm's status. The evidence is not supportive of this theory as the FTC found that "conglomerate firms were not inclined to acquire failing firms. In 1967 and 1968 conglomerates did not acquire a single

loser. . . ."[18] Indeed, in May, 1978, data presented in an article in Barrons showed that conglomerates were acquiring only very profitable
companies. "A major attraction of the takeovers
seemed to be above-average profitability. . . .
The return on average equity (of 70 takeover firms)
. . . was an above average 16.2% to 14.0% for
Standard and Poor's 400."[19] Finally, evidence presented by Robert Conn in 1976 indicated that "the
acquired firms are not (the) faltering (type)."[20]
All these studies suggest that the healthy firm
seeking the failing firm hypothesis is invalid.

The second possibility is that failing firms
seek healthy firms and thereby diversify to survive. This route would be taken in lieu of going
out of business either voluntarily or through
bankruptcy; the failing firm would be opting to
maintain the longevity of the firm, albeit in different product markets. The existing data is inconclusive. A study by Peter Dodd and Richard
Ruback showed that conglomerates which had been
successful bidders tended to outperform the stock
market during the years before their acquisitions
were made.[21] In addition, Conn studying conglomerate mergers which occurred between 1960 and 1968,
found that firms of similar profitability tended
to merge and that, in general, a great deal of
financial vitality was exhibited by acquirers as
well as by acquirees.[22]

However, J. Fred Weston and Surendra Mansinghka
studied the financial characteristics of conglomerate firms as they related to the same characteristics of the firms acquired in the period 1958-1968
and found that the conglomerates had a lower profit
rate than the acquired firms. This led them to conclude that the defensive diversification/failing
firm argument was supported by the evidence.
"Analysis of the backgrounds and acquisition his-
tories of the conglomerate firms suggests that
they were diversifying defensively to avoid (1)
sales and profit instability, (2) adverse growth
developments, (3) adverse competition shifts, (4)
technological obsolescence."[23] Support of the
Weston-Mansinghka position is found in the work of
Ronald Melicher and David Rush. Their study of
conglomerate acquisitions in the period 1960-1969
shows that the conglomerates had significantly
lower operating profit levels than the firms they
acquired.[24] They suggest that their findings are

"consistent with the defensive diversification
. . . hypothesis formulated by Weston and Mansinghka."[25] Since there is disagreement in the
literature on this point as of this writing, the
only conclusion that can be drawn is that the
defensive motive is a possible reason for diversification.

The third possibility is that healthy firms
seek healthy firms and presumes that the price of
the stock of the acquired firm is not as great as
would be consistent with an intrinsic valuation.
Therefore diversification takes place because the
conglomerate values a particular firm more than
the market values it. While it may be that defensive diversification was responsible for diversification in the 1960s, the same may not be true
in the 1970s. These years have been characterized
by conglomerate "takeovers," many of which were
not received kindly (hostile mergers).[26] Usually,
hostility exists when the acquired firm is very
secure and profitable, and when it regards its
autonomy to be important if not paramount. The
term "bargain hunting" is sometimes used in
instances like these where there appears to be an
incentive for firms to diversify in order to get
more than what they offer. This could be a reason
for a new wave of diversification to have evolved
in the late 1970s.[27]

Another explanation which can account for the
surge in conglomerate activity involves staying
power. The larger the firm, the more capable it
will be to withstand economic downturns, regardless of their severity. There are two issues involved here. First, the larger its amount of
assets, the more capable a firm is of borrowing
money, retrenching in the marketplace, and sus-
taining losses over a given period of time. Smaller
firms operate with less assets and credit than
larger firms, hence, during a crunch, they are the
first to have their lines of credit withdrawn. The
larger the firm, the longer the period of time
before any credit problems will arise and, as a
rule, large firms can be expected to weather most
downturns without too much credit pressure.

The second issue involves the reduction of risk
which refers to the probability of loss associated
with business investments; it is measured by the
variance of earnings. Classical portfolio theory
rests on the premise that risk can be minimized

through diversification.[28] A conglomerate, by becoming active in many diverse markets, can reduce
the risk associated with having all of its resources in a single market. Through diversification, a conglomerate may be able to realize profits in markets which it would otherwise not have
been involved, thereby offsetting any unexpected
losses in other markets. Possibly the greater the
number of markets a conglomerate serves, and the
more unrelated these markets are to one another,
the more stable its earnings will be over a period
of time.

    Consider an example of a firm which produces
two products.[29] Let σ_1 and σ_2 be the standard de-
viations of earnings in Markets 1 and 2 respec-
tively. Then, the standard deviation of the firm's
total profits can be expressed by σ_t where

$$\sigma_t = \sqrt{\sigma_1^2 + \sigma_2^2 + 2r\sigma_1\sigma_2}$$

and r is the correlation coefficient of profits in
the two markets. When the products in Market 1 and
2 are perfect complements, that is, there is perfect positive correlation, $r = 1$. Here it is easy
to see that σ_t reaches its maximum possible value.
Profits will oscillate between being very high and
very low since a decline in Market 1 will be
accompanied by a decline in Market 2 and conversely. This is the antithesis of risk reduction
through diversification. If Markets 1 and 2
exhibit perfect negative correlation, as would be
the case if the products were perfect substitutes,
$r = -1$, then when profits in one market go up by,
say, 10%, there will be an equal offsetting
decline in the other market. This would be the
case of perfect risk reduction, but, practically
speaking, it would not be the expected result of
conglomerate mergers.

    A conglomerate, seeking to reduce risk, would
place itself in two totally unrelated markets.
Here, with $r = 0$, the standard deviation is
smaller. As Scherer has noted, "the more markets
with randomly related profits the conglomerate
serves, ceteris paribus, the more its risk will
be spread, and the smaller will be the standard
deviation of total profits in relation to average

total profits."[30] Thus, while perfect risk reduction is not generally achievable, diversification
should result in a reduction of risk.

A novel approach to the discussion of conglomerate diversification and risk focuses on the position of the lender of funds who has the choice of
loaning to a conglomerate or a nonconglomerate.
Using the assumption that the lender wants to mini-
mize the risk of default on the loan, Wilbur
Lewellan found that "the likelihood of default is
reduced when firms combine . . . (therefore) a
merged corporation (conglomerate) must be more
attractive to . . . the supplier of debt."[31] This
lends support to the postulate that diversification reduces earnings instability. The assured
stability of earnings makes conglomerates more
attractive to a lender of funds.

A second approach used in measuring the degree
of risk reduction associated with diversification
focuses on stock market prices. For analytical and
measurement purposes, risk can be separated into
two components: systematic and unsystematic.[32]
Systematic risk refers to the risk that is present
due to the variability of all stock prices taken
together.[33] Unsystematic risk is attributed to
factors peculiar to the particular firm such as
labor strikes and fire damage. Systematic risk
cannot be reduced; it is the measure of uncertainty
that is built into the stock market itself. However, the standard capital asset pricing model
demonstrates that diversification can reduce unsystematic risk and that perfect diversification
can virtually eliminate it.[34] Figure 2.2 is a
helpful guide in conceptualizing this. In essence,
a program of diversification can reduce total risk
to systematic risk.

One needs to ascertain whether corporate
diversification has, in fact, reduced total risk.
For this purpose a measure called beta has been
devised.[35] Beta measures the volitility of a
firm's stock price relative to swings in the stock
market. That is, it measures to what extent a
firm's stock price rises and falls as the general
market rises and falls. For instance, suppose beta
equals 0.10 for a particular stock. Then if the
market swings up by some magnitude, this stock's
price will swing up by 10% of that.

Very few studies have been done regarding risk
and conglomerate diversification. Randolph Wester-

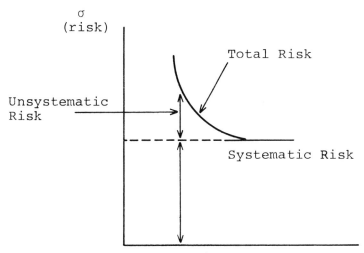

Fig. 2.2. How diversification reduces risk

SOURCE: Burton Malkiel, A Random Walk Down Wall
Street (New York: Norton, 1975), p. 189.

field tested the hypothesis that conglomerate
diversification reduces (eliminates) unsystematic
risk. In comparing conglomerates to mutual funds
(near perfect diversification exists here), he
found that conglomerates are not as successful as
mutual funds in reducing risk.[36] However, for the
periods studied, 1954-1961 and 1961-1968, he
found that conglomerates had been successful in
reducing unsystematic risk. That is, while they
have not been as efficient as mutual funds, they
have reduced this component of risk.[37] This find-
ing is not surprising as Oliver Williamson notes:

> If a conglomerate has as its purpose a risk-
> pooling agency--it will be inferior to mutual
> funds--because the transaction costs associ-
> ated with altering the composition of the
> portfolio of the conglomerate--by selling of
> existing divisions and acquiring new operat-
> ing companies, will ordinarily exceed the
> costs that a mutual fund of comparable assets
> would incur in trading its common stock.[38]

Melicher and Rush traced the performance of
conglomerate and nonconglomerate firms in reducing

risk.[39] Their results suggest that conglomerates
have not succeeded in performing in a superior
manner relative to nonconglomerates. First, they
note that conglomerate firms had higher betas
than their nonconglomerate counterparts.[40] For the
capital-asset pricing model to hold, it must follow that in "up" markets, the conglomerate firms
should outperform their counterparts. This was not
found to be the case. Not only did they find that
the betas were higher, but the expected higher
returns were not forthcoming.[41] In addition, they
found that the average standard deviation of investment returns of conglomerates was greater than
the nonconglomerate firms. Finally, they found
that, while conglomerate firms had achieved a
higher degree of diversification, they had
achieved no significant difference in risk-rate of
return performance.[42] Their final conclusion was
that "conglomerate diversification . . . does not
seem to be an effective vehicle for obtaining
superior or outstanding performance."[43]

The empirical work done in the area of risk
reduction through diversification is inconclusive.
Therefore, if a firm is diversifying because of
its desire to reduce risk, it must be basing its
decision on the implications of risk reduction
theory, not empirical evidence.

Berle and Means noted long ago that a firm's
incorporation would necessarily transform its
character from that of owner-manager oneness to
owner-manager separateness.[44] They suggested that
managers' interests became separate from those of
the owners (stockholders) in that the owners were
interested in profit-maximization, stock price
appreciation, and increased dividends, while managers were interested in personal utility maximization which converts into maximizing salaries,
emoluments, and status. Thus, managers and owners
should be expected to have different views as to
what the firm's objectives ought to be. Richard
Cyert and James March have questioned whether a
theory of the firm should assume that firms strive
to maximize profits.[45] They suggest, as did Berle
and Means, that managers may maximize their own
utility and thus sacrifice profit maximization.
Indeed, management decisions to diversify may be a
function of their own utility needs. This would
follow particularly if conglomerate firms do tend
to confer higher salaries, emoluments, and status

on management than do other forms of corporate
structure.

William Baumol supports the belief that managers trade off profit maximization for the goals
listed above.[46] He proposes that managers attempt
to maximize total revenue, not profits. This follows in the sense that sales rather than profits
may be regarded as a better indicator of the
vitality and health of a firm (assuming some positive rate of profit is earned).[47] "So long as
profits are high enough to keep stockholders satisfied and contribute adequately to the financing of
company growth, management will bend its efforts
to the augmentation of sales revenue rather than
to further increases in profit."[48]

Baumol's model is presented in Figure 2.3. If
the profit rate required to keep stockholders
satisfied is low, say as π_1, then maximum revenue
can be obtained at output Q_s. Here the rate of
profit is P_s which is greater than π_1, therefore
the firm can maximize revenue without constraint.
However, if the required profit rate is π_2, then
sales will have to be reduced to Q_c where the
profit rate, P_s', is equal to π_2. Baumol is sug-
gesting that stockholder interests and solvency
determine the degree of constraint that management
feels in maximizing revenue. This fits nicely into
a theory which seeks to explain the motivation for
diversification. Managers who pursue diversification may actually be seeking a way to maximize the
revenue of the firm.

Carl Kaysen has maintained that manager's
motives are distinct from shareholders' and that
the divergent interests would translate into the
desires of the stockholders being placed second
to the needs (goals) of the managers.[49] Robert
Gordon, Herbert Simon, and Samuel Reid, agreeing
with Kaysen, Baumol, and Berle and Means, have
suggested that the personal utility goals of
security, power, prestige, increased income, and
advancement of management would take precedence
over corporate profits.[50]

In testing this hypothesis, Joseph McGuire,
John Chui, and Alvar Elbing found a valid relationship between executive salaries and sales
revenue of the firm; their results indicated no
significant relationship between executive incomes
and profits.[51] They observed that there seemed to
be a causality factor that ran from sales to

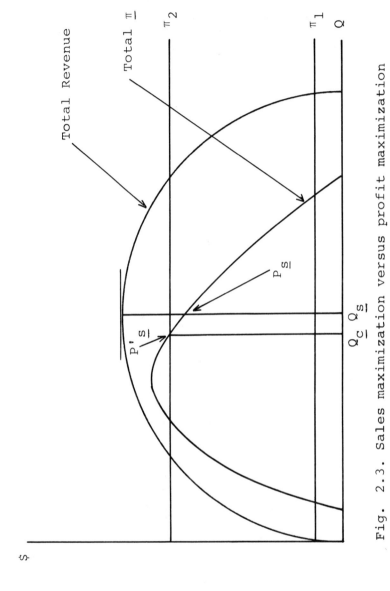

Fig. 2.3. Sales maximization versus profit maximization

SOURCE: William Baumol, Business Behavior, Value and Growth (New York: Harcourt, 1967), p. 54.

salaries since increases in sales in previous
periods--as well as in current periods--seemed to
be rewarded by higher salaries. Williamson found
that management did not have a neutral attitude
toward costs: "directly or indirectly, certain
classes of expenditures have positive values
associated with them, that is, staff expenses and
expenditures for emoluments" (fraction of managerial salaries and perquisites that are discretionary).[52] Since growth through diversification automatically increases the total sales of the firm,
management attitudes toward diversification, like
attitudes toward costs, may not be neutral.

Reid followed a similar approach but added the
dimension of risk and security to the analysis.[53]
He argued that the assured continuity of a firm
reduces the risk associated with a manager's position thereby conferring on the manager a sense of
personal security. Thus, Reid postulated that
growth through diversification should lead to
increases in profits as well as sheer size if, in
fact, managers and owner-stockholder interests are
the same. The results of his work indicated that
increases in growth through merger enhanced managements' interests (sales, assets, and number of
employees), while it decreased owner-stockholder
interests (price of stock and profit to original
stockholders). He concluded "the more actively a
firm merges, the more it tends to further managers'
interests rather than stockholders'."[54] Interest-
ingly, Reid found that conglomerate growth, relative to horizontal, vertical, or internal, was the
most likely to be associated with size maximization rather than profit maximization. Thus, conglomerate growth tended to be the most supportive
of management objectives.

Management may have another motive for growth
and diversification. Berle and Means suggested
that incorporation leads to a diffuseness of ownership which allows control of the firm to slip
into the hands of a few. Since it is the board of
directors that has legal control of the firm,
Berle and Means argued that the real control of an
enterprise lies with the group which has the power
to select the board.[55] If management wants control, they must control the board. Five types of
control exist, three legal and two extra legal.[56]
The three legal types are control through complete
ownership of the stock of a firm, majority owner-

ship, and other legal devices such as voting trusts
or special classes of voting stock. The two extra
legal types are minority control and management
control. Minority control occurs when an individual or small group holds such a sufficient block
that it can gain majority control with the help of
a scattering of proxies. The classic case often
cited is the Rockefeller-Stewart fight for control
of Standard Oil of Indiana. Rockefeller, a minority
stockholder, was able to wrest control from Stewart,
the management representative of the firm, by getting sufficient proxy support.[57]

Management control is most likely to occur when
ownership is so widely dispersed that no individual or small group has a sufficient minority interest that can be turned into a majority vote.
Conglomerates fit nicely into this category. As
they expand and diversify, ownership is increasingly dispersed, and management control becomes
much more likely. In these circumstances, control
of the firm will go to those who control the election of the board of directors.[58] If management
appoints the proxy committee which selects the
board members (who generally run unopposed for
election), then management has virtual control of
the firm. The great diffuseness of the voting
shareholders makes the proxy vote the assured
winner.

As a firm grows and diversifies, there are in-
dications that a set of management objectives are
enhanced. Larger firms tend to give managers
higher salaries, more perquisites and staff, more
prestige, and increased security. It also allows
for management autonomy in those cases where ownership is widely dispersed. Managements' goals and
well-being, then, may be an important factor which
helps explain the emergence of large, conglomerate
firms.

Corwin Edwards hypothesized that large, diversified firms have a greater ability to price a product below cost for a sustained period of time
relative to smaller, less diversified firms.[59] His
argument is based on the concept of deep pockets;
that is, that the large, diversified firms have
the power to spend money in large amounts. The
length of the purse makes it easy to match losses
with smaller, less diversified firms. In a price
war, the large diversified firm would be the vic-
tor.[60] For the deep pockets theory to hold, at

least a few of the markets that the conglomerate
firm faces must be imperfectly competitive and
continuously earning economic profits. Obviously,
the more imperfect these markets, the higher the
rates of profit. The cross-subsidization concept
follows from the deep pockets theory as it refers
to the ability of the firm to use economic profits
from a less competitive market to subsidize below
cost pricing in a more competitive market. Edwards'
argument is that large, diversified firms, facing
at least some imperfect markets, are in a better
position to enter new markets, to increase market
share in already existing markets, to discipline
rivals whose pricing policies are deemed inconsistent with its own, and to defend any and all
markets from attack.[61] Deep pockets, potential
cross-subsidization, and all associated benefits
could provide an incentive for diversification.

Pricing below cost to drive out competitors,
eliminate potential competitors, and discipline
competitors have long been considered options for
oligopolists. In the present discussion, this concept is broadened to the extent that the conglomerate firm can use resources from other markets
to fund the economic pressure being brought on
another market. There is no question that the
deep-pockets-cross-subsidization theory is plausi-
ble. However, the evidence that is available does
not clearly demonstrate that it is a popular device.

Donald Turner has analyzed this and concluded
that "the belief that predatory pricing is a
likely consequence of conglomerate size, and hence
of conglomerate merger, is wholly unverified by
any careful studies; research and analysis suggest
that in all likelihood this belief is just
wrong."[62] Turner's strong statement is based upon
his belief, shared by Scherer and others, that
regardless of the depth of the long purse, pricing
below cost will not be considered unless the firm
can also establish significant barriers to entry
against new firms after the old firms are driven
from the market or reduced in size.[63] If barriers
cannot be erected, the loss during the pricing-
below-cost period probably cannot be recouped
afterwards. If barriers do not exist prior to this
pricing strategy (they did not, by definition,
since a fringe of competitors must have existed
for this pricing strategy to be warranted), the

elimination of competitors alone would not be sufficient to reward the effort.

There are other possible explanations why a
conglomerate may price a product 'low' or below
cost. First, it may be that a conglomerate firm's
management may not be motivated to maximize profits. Managements' goals may be such that price is
lower than the maximum the market will bear,
therefore sales can be maximized instead. Second,
conglomerate firms may not want to give up traditional markets even though demand is such that
losses are incurred. Finally, the firm may choose
to offer a product as a loss leader.

These explanations not withstanding, there have
been cases documented in which deep pockets and
cross-subsidization have come into play either to
discipline a rival or increase a conglomerate's
market share in a particular market. The Safeway
Store chain provides an example of disciplining
rivals. In order to dissuade its rivals in the
Texas region from issuing trading stamps, Safeway
initiated a vigorous price war in that area. "Over
a fifteen month period the price-cutting stores
recorded losses of $4 million on sales of roughly
$230 million while profits in other regional
divisions remained healthy."[64] Subsequently, the
widespread issuance of trading stamps in that area
was halted.

An example of increasing market share is found
in the case of National Dairy Products Corporation.[65] In 1960 National was the twentieth largest industrial firm in the United States, having,
as one of its divisions, Kraft Foods. Kraft's
sales of jams and jellies amounted to 5.9% of a
particular eastern market. This figure constituted
3.5% of Kraft's national sales and 0.03% of
National Dairy Products' total sales. The market
was dominated by regional firms with Old Virginia
having 15.8% and T. Friedman 11.9%.

Early in 1961, Kraft decided to increase its
market share by offering a free case of jam or
jelly with every case purchased, essentially a 50%
reduction in price. As a result, Kraft sold twice
as many cases in a twenty-six-day period in 1961
as it had in all of 1960. The FTC later showed
that this two-for-the-price-of-one offer meant
that jams and jellies had been sold at a price
which did not cover production cost. The regional
competitors did not meet Kraft's price reduction.

They indicated that they could not sustain that
price for any period of time and that their only
choice was to sell less at a higher price. The
president of Old Virginia said that following
Kraft would have resulted in bankruptcy.

The FTC charged National Dairy with anticompetitive behavior and upon review the Seventh Court
of Appeals stated that "The cost was of necessity
subsidized from income by . . . National Dairy in
its operations elsewhere. . . . The Commission was
warranted in inferring that . . . (National Dairy's
losses in the market areas were made up from its
treasury, in turn obtained from sales elsewhere."[66]

The takeover of Miller Brewing by Philip Morris
provides another example of increasing market
share. In 1970, before the takeover, Miller sold
5.1 million barrels of beer. After the takeover,
this figure grew such that in 1978, 30 million
barrels were sold.[67] This moved Miller from a low
market share position in 1970 to a position of
second behind Anheuser-Busch in 1978.[68] Miller's
success was derived from three sources: a change
in image, new product lines, and extensive advertising.[69] These actions were made possible by
Philip Morris' long purse.

One firm's access to cross-subsidization from a
conglomerate may induce other firms to seek the
protection of a conglomerate umbrella. A single-
product firm competing with other single-product
firms need not be concerned with cross-subsidization. But as soon as one of those firms becomes a
part of a conglomerate, the others feel the threat
of unequal competition; self-defense dictates that
they become a part of another diversified firm.
This occurred in the food industry in 1965 when
National Biscuit Company was considering a merger
with Coca Cola. The Sunshine Biscuit Company,
National's competitor, then decided to consider
merging with American Tobacco. As one director of
Sunshine said:

> While there has been a tendency toward lack
> of interest in proposals of consolidation
> in the past, the recent reports of NBC and
> Coca Cola, although now called off, would
> in my opinion justify our careful consider-
> ation of this offer (from American Tobacco)
> which appears to be more to the general in-
> terest and advantage of our stock-holders

than any of the previous offers we have
received--at least it appears so to me
from the information I can recall having
received.

It seems definitely certain that if our
competitor with an already larger advertising budget than ours should join with
someone with a similar advantage--that we
could be snowed under in this field, much
to the detriment of our future sales and
profits.[70]

Growth through diversification requires consideration of ways to enter new markets, to increase
one's share in existing markets, and to discipline
rivals and survive their attacks. The deep pock-
ets-cross-subsidization advantage may give a firm
the incentive to diversify. The deep pockets idea,
itself, is not unlike the notion of staying power
and risk reduction. Coupled with the possibility
of cross-subsidization, it can become an offensive
weapon as well as a defensive strategy.

The existence of a reciprocal buying agreement
between two firms, say, A and B, means that Firm A
agrees to purchase goods from Firm B as long as
Firm B grants Firm A some type of concession. This
concession could take several forms. Firm B might
reduce its price for Firm A; Firm B might agree to
purchase goods from Firm A; Firm B might put pressure on a third firm, C, to deal with Firm A. A
careful reading of Purchasing Magazine over the
past two decades indicates that reciprocity is
practiced in the economy; larger firms tend to be
more active in reciprocal dealings than smaller
firms; and firms in the oil and chemical industries
are especially likely to engage in reciprocal dealings.[71] The concern here is about whether opportunities for reciprocity provide an incentive for
diversification.

Conglomerates are in the unique position of
producing many products. This means they could
direct certain of their subsidiaries to deal
exclusively, or in large part, with other subsidiaries when buying and selling products. By inter-
nalizing these transactions, a conglomerate may
gain advantage through price savings or through
reducing excess capacity. Regarding external purchases, a firm may be enticed to diversify in
order to have the opportunity to practice reciproc-

ity. The more products a firm offers, the larger
the number of opportunities it has. Also, reciprocity can be quite advantageous to a firm producing
a homogeneous product, for it allows the firm a
way of reducing the degree of competitiveness it
faces in the marketplace.

A reciprocal arrangement between two firms may
be either mutual or coercive. Mutual refers to a
situation where the two firms enter into a reciprocal pact that benefits both firms. Coercive, on
the other hand, refers to an arrangement where one
firm gains from the other. Consider the following:
Firm A, a large, diversified firm buys a substantial amount of Firm B's product. Firm B is a small
firm in a competitive industry. Firm A can use its
large buying power to wrest price concessions from
Firm B. If Firm B refuses to submit to the pressure, then Firm A can change its buying pattern.
This is coercive reciprocity: I will buy from you
if you lower your price. Economic power on the
side of the conglomerate can facilitate this concession.

Another type of concession involves a less
powerful firm buying from a conglomerate. The conglomerate may suggest that the firm buy several of
its products instead of only one. The more diversified the firm, the higher the probability that a
buyer can use more than one of the conglomerate's
products. Several often mentioned examples of
reciprocity are included below to illustrate how
it works.

In the late 1950s General Dynamics, a conglomerate, acquired Liquid Carbonic. At the time of the
takeover General Dynamics indicated that it was
motivated by a desire to reduce its dependency on
government demand so that it could become more
active in the private sector. Liquid Carbonic
viewed the move quite differently, as the following statement by its president indicates.

If my information is correct, Liquid's management would have at its disposal the
entire purchasing power of General Dynamics'
other Divisions for reciprocal business purposes. During this period of rapidly increasing competition and recognizing that Liquid's
sales force is woefully weak, the advantage
of this reciprocity would be of unlimited
value in getting a load on our plants both

old and new. . . . If, through reciprocity,
we would put a load on all our plants on a
year-round basis, our earnings would rise
very rapidly.

This opportunity is available to us now. If
we reject it, General Dynamics will deal
with one of our competitors. . . . Based on
the experience I have had . . . I would hate
to face one of our major competitors if he
were to have at his disposal the tremendous
purchasing power of General Dynamics to be
used as a reciprocal instrument of sales.[72]
(Italics added.)

An internal auditor for one of the major conglomerates testified in 1973,

In every division and subsidiary I've examined
in the past 4 months, the pattern is the
same. Purchase after purchase of items like
office equipment, furniture, and kitchen
equipment for cafeterias has been made from
other divisions of this company that make
these items--and I find no evidence that
competitive bids were ever asked for.[73]

In 1975, Consolidated Foods Corporation and
National Tea Company were involved in competition
in the supermarket industry. Consolidated Foods
was a large producer of baked goods (Sara Lee) and
also operated a few small supermarkets in the
Chicago area. National Tea had 237 supermarkets in
Chicago and carried Sara Lee products bought from
Consolidated Foods. When Consolidated cut prices
in its few supermarkets, National suffered a loss
of revenue at its stores. National Tea decided
that it would no longer carry Consolidated Foods'
baked goods at its 237 retail outlets. Since this
was Consolidated's primary economic interest
(supermarkets being secondary), it was decided
that the price-cutting campaign at the supermarkets
must be abandoned. National Tea then resumed order-
ing baked goods from Consolidated. Ultimately,
Consolidated sold the few supermarkets it owned in
Chicago.[74]
A powerful conglomerate may be able to use an
external intermediary, usually a financial institution, to pressure a third party to do business

with it. The case of American Standard Corporation
illustrates this. American Standard was a large,
diversified firm in 1960. It had created a commercial relations department to coordinate aspects of
selling, buying, and financing. It routinely designated several banks to serve as depositories for
tax funds with the understanding

> Banks could reciprocate in four ways: they
> could require that American products be used
> in buildings for which the bank had full re-
> sponsibility; they could influence the pur-
> chase decisions of the third parties by, at
> least, expressing their satisfaction with
> American products; they could augment a
> rather imperfect information system by pro-
> viding advance information of projects and
> responsible parties, and they could perform
> the useful "introducing" function by over-
> coming difficulties experienced in gaining
> entree to an engineering or building firm.[75]

Another example involves Consolidated Foods and
its acquisition, in 1951, of Gentry, a manufacturer
of dehydrated onions and garlic.[76] Since Consolidated was a leading purchaser of soup, on occasion
it would try to use this leverage to get soup producers to buy from Gentry. These efforts were
rarely successful.

A final example involves the acquisition by ITT
of Canteen Corporation in 1969. This acquisition
exemplifies how structural arrangements can lead
to potential reciprocity. In 1969 ITT made purchases of more than $100,000 from 61 of the larg-
est 100 manufacturing firms in the economy. Canteen, on the other hand, sold vended and manual
food to these same firms. Therefore this merger
made these firms the customer of ITT just as ITT
was their customer. Obvious opportunities for
reciprocal arrangements were facilitated by this
structural arrangement.[77]

Reciprocity is a practiced art in the manufacturing sector of the economy. The data indicate
that the larger and more diversified is the firm,
the more likely it is to be engaged in reciprocal
dealings. The obvious advantage of practicing
reciprocity could be the reduction of either
excess capacity or input costs. There is evidence
that conglomerates have practiced this art in the

past and that, in some instances, reciprocity provided a motive for diversification. It must be
considered as one possible explanation for the
emergence of conglomerates.

Earnings per share of stock are considered to
be a barometer of a firm's well-being while the
price-earnings (P/E) ratio reflects the public's
confidence in the earning power of the stock. A
high P/E ratio signifies that a firm is likely to
have above average earnings over the long-run.
Thus, investors will buy this stock with the ex-
pectation of price appreciation as the expected
increased earnings materialize. Firms can use
their P/E ratios to enhance their earnings per
share by acquiring firms that have different P/E
ratios.

If one firm acquires another firm having a
lower P/E ratio, the acquirer can automatically
raise its earnings per share without either of the
firms actually experiencing an increase in earnings. The converse also holds. The following
example illustrates this.

Assume the existence of 3 firms--the
acquirer (A) and 2 acquired firms (B and C).
Each has an income of $1,000, 2 shares, and
earnings per share of $500; the only differ-
ence is in the P/E ratios: A has a ratio of
14 to 1, B has a ratio of 7 to 1, and C has
a ratio of 21 to 1.

Before Acquisition

	Income	Number of Shares	Earnings per Share	P/E Ratio	Price per Share
Company A	$1,000	2	$500	14 to 1	$ 7,000
Company B	1,000	2	500	7 to 1	3,500
Company C	1,000	2	500	21 to 1	10,500

After Acquisition

Company B	2,000	3	667
Company C	2,000	5	400

A can acquire B by issuing just one additional
share, the owners of the latter agreeing to
exchange their 2 shares worth $3,500 each for

one share of A's stock worth $7,000. A's in-
come will double as a result of absorbing B
but its number of shares will increase only
from 2 to 3. Hence its earnings per share
will rise from $500 to $667. To acquire C,
however, A will have to issue 3 new shares
of stock, the owners of C exchanging their
2 shares worth $10,500 each for 3 shares
of A worth $7,000 each. Added to its ori-
ginal 2 shares A will have 5 shares outstanding, giving it an earnings per share of
$400 as compared to its pre-acquisition fig-
ure of $500.[78]

Conglomerate firms have traditionally been
labeled growth companies since they have been in
the business of acquiring other firms. In many
instances their P/E ratios are higher than most
other publically traded firms and the opportunity
to raise earnings through continued diversification is always present. Walter Mead compared the
P/E ratios of acquiring the acquired firms in
1967-68 for conglomerate mergers. He found that
"conglomerate mergers are characterized as cases
in which there is a price-earnings differential
favorable to the acquiring firm."[79] What actually
happened in the late 1960s was that the conglomerate acquired very mature firms in mature industries. These were the firms with lower P/E ratios.
Firms in steel-making, machine tools, pumps, rail
equipment, and the like became the prime targets
for takeovers.[80]
    Once a firm establishes the reputation of being
a growth firm, its P/E ratio should rise above
that of the other firms in the market. Since an
increase in earnings is universally welcomed by
owners, managers, and debt holders alike, growth
through diversification may be caused by the opportunity to increase earnings in this fashion.
    Whereas, the maxim, 'the whole is equal to the
sum of its parts' was once considered a truism,
synergy now provides that the whole may exceed the
sum of the parts. Stated another way, two plus two
may in fact equal five. Given the existing tax
laws and generally accepted accounting practices,
when two firms combine to form one firm, the
result may be that the new firm shows greater
profits than the sum of the profits of the two
original firms. Accounting rules regarding pooling

and goodwill were changed by the Accounting Principles Board of the American Institute of Certified Public Accountants in August, 1970. The new rule, known as Opinion 16, makes it more difficult to use these techniques. For a detailed analysis of Opinion 16, see Fred Weston and Eugene Brigham, Essentials of Managerial Finance, 3d ed. (Hinsdale, Ill., The Dryden Press, 1974), chap. 23.

When two entities, say, a conglomerate and another firm, merge, the assets of the two are added together or, to use the vernacular, pooled. What frequently happens is that the conglomerate adds only the book value of the acquired company's assets to its own. The book value is usually less than the price paid by the conglomerate, and this results in an understatement of the investment made. Consequently the rate of return on capital shown at the end of the fiscal period is automatically increased. For example, suppose conglomerate ABC which has a book value of $100 buys Firm Q which has a book value of $50. Also suppose ABC pays $75 for Q. If, in the next accounting period, ABC shows a profit of $10, and one uses the pooled book value--$100 + $50 = $150, then the rate of return is $10/$150 or 6.67%. However, if the value had been computed as $100 + $75 = $175, then the rate of return would have been $10/$175 = 5.7%. So, although there is no real difference, the apparent difference is rather significant. Litton Industries, a conglomerate, provides a case in point.

> Litton Industries suppressed $80 million in costs when it pooled with American Book and Jefferson Electric Company during its fiscal year ending July 31, 1967. These values, "which presumably have produced or will produce revenues for Litton over the years, have not entered into such statements. As a result the corporation's earnings will be exaggerated over the years by the amount thus suppressed." With pooling and other devices for cost suppression in widespread use, it is surprising that merger-active companies as a class do not inevitably indicate superior profitability by whatever measure used.[81]

Another device often used is that of charging
the difference between the book value and the
actual amount paid to goodwill. The key here is
that goodwill is not an asset that is amortized or
charged to any other account. It may remain on the
books as a separate category with the result that
it becomes, effectively, a suppressed item. Again,
the rate of return is overstated and synergy is
achieved.

The example of pyramiding in chapter 1 showed
that voting control of a corporation could be
gained with a "small" investment. Analogously,
leverage provides that bonds and preferred stock
used to buy firms can work to increase earnings
per share of common stock. What happens is that
the acquired firm's earnings are added to the conglomerate's earnings but its assets are not. This
automatically increases the earnings per share of
the conglomerate's common stock. Consider the
example of Ling-Temco-Vought.

LTV's acquisition of Wilson & Co., the
meatpacker, illustrates the use of leverage.
LTV paid so large a premium for this acquisition that it made Wilsons' price-earnings
ratio higher than LTV's. Yet, LTV realized
an immediate earnings gain. The acquisition
increased LTV's earnings per share by 31
percent, from $4.32 to $5.68. Before the
announcement of the acquisition, Wilson's
price-earnings ratio was 9.0, substantially
less than LTV's ratio of 17.2; however, LTV
paid a 108 percent premium for Wilson,
thereby raising Wilson's price-earnings
ratio to 18.5. By issuing no new shares of
common stock, LTV utilized the maximum possible amount of leverage by paying for this
acquisition with about $144 million in cumu-
lative preferred stock and $81.5 million in
cash, $80 million of which was financed with
debt instruments.[82]

Like P/E ratios, suppressed items and leverage are
techniques that can be used to give the appearance
of increased earnings when no actual increase has
taken place. These may provide incentive for
growth through diversification.

There are numerous financial benefits which may
accrue to a conglomerate when it acquires another

firm. One pertains to pension funds. Most firms
have pension funds set up for their employees and,
in some cases, these funds are of substantial size.
If a conglomerate can enhance the size of its pension fund through merger, it can reduce its contributions to the fund for some time to come. During this period the firm may allocate the freed
funds for other capital uses. One obvious use
would be the acquisition of other firms.[83] The
American Standard-Mullins Manufacturing attempted
merger provides an example. Mullins had built up a
pension fund in excess of $5 million, which, dur-
ing the merger with American Standard, was combined with Standard's pension fund. The merger was
subsequently disallowed and when the unscrambling
took place, the original $5 million became $0.5
million, Standard kept $4.5 million.[84]

Another type of financial benefit accrues to
conglomerates which acquire firms having hidden
assets. Hidden assets are usually the result of
years of painstaking husbanding of assets. Con-
servative accounting practices assuring liquidity,
low indebtedness, and ample depreciation charges
leave a firm with a lackluster yet solid and finan-
cially respectable performance record. Firms with
hidden assets are attractive to diversifying firms
because of the obvious opportunity to show percip-
itous increases in earnings. A case in point is
the Gulf and Western acquisition of Paramount Pic-
tures. The managers of Gulf and Western recognized
Paramount's library of films which had not previously been rented out as a wealth of hidden assets.
A. Briloff observed,

> To the head of Gulf and Western, acquiring
> Paramount was like 'buying a bank' . . . the
> G&W management was able to assert . . . that
> while tired old Paramount had earned less
> than $3 million the year before the take-
> over, in the less than a year immediately
> following its getting the pool with G&W,
> it was able to earn more than 7 times that
> sum--over $22 million. . . . Overlooked was
> the fact that G&W was doing nothing more
> than stripping the top soil which was so
> carefully nurtured by the traditional Para-
> mount management and proceeding to sell this
> fertile soil.[85]

Finally, there is the tax incentive. Today's
tax laws allow corporations to carry over losses
from previous fiscal periods as tax credits against
current earnings. When a firm has large current
losses and little expectations of high earnings in
the future, it has no opportunity to use the tax
law to its own advantage. It might thus be induced
to diversify into profitable lines so that a tax
savings could be realized. It has been suggested
that Textron had this incentive during the decade
1953-1962, when it made 39 acquisitions.[86] Textron's annual sales rose from $71 million to $550
million during this period; in addition, it sold
(at a loss) either whole or parts of enterprises
which had been acquired. The FTC's position was
that "Textron's tax losses were a major factor in
motivating its growth by merger, in building up a
glamorous reputation for growth of sales and earnings, and in financing many of its mergers."[87]
Thus the lure of financial benefits, be they obvious or hidden, cannot be discounted as a motive
for diversification.

The motives for diversification seem to fit
into two categories: defensive and offensive. Defensive actions taken by firms assure their survival, size and profitability. In this category we
find such motives as the failing firm, staying
power and risk reduction, management control and
some facets of cross-subsidization. Offensive
motives provide the firm the opportunity to remain
healthy; they include cost reduction, reciprocity,
other facets of cross-subsidization, and exploita-
tion of potential financial benefits.

These two categories not withstanding, there
appears to be a common denominator, namely endur-
ance, which binds these motives together. Regardless of the rationale for diversification, longevity is the desired outcome; firms diversify in
order to endure in an ever changing economic system.

3 Firm Diversification and Economic Structure

THIS CHAPTER assesses the degree of diversification that exists in the manufacturing sector of the economy today and identifies those firms which are the most diversified. The focus is on the two hundred largest manufacturing firms (based on asset size, a study of the 1977 Annual Reports as filed with the Security and Exchange Commission [SEC], and the asset list of Fortune 500 of May 1977) that control two-thirds of the assets of the manufacturing sector. The underlying reason for estimating the degree of diversification is to increase one's information regarding the structure of this sector. As noted, diversification allows firms more options of behavior (reciprocity, cross-subsidization, etc.) than those of a single product firm. In addition, where several large, conglomerate firms exist and interact in a set of markets, their conduct options are constrained by more than the circumstances surrounding any one of those markets.[1] These firms must adjust their behavior given the web of markets in which they interact; what results is constrained, noncompeting behavior. This, of course, is Corwin Edwards' spheres of influence hypothesis.[2] The question that arises is whether the degree of diversification that exists has placed these firms in webs of markets that would be conducive to this type of behavior.

A systematic evaluation of diversification will be facilitated by the use of the Standard Industrial Classification (SIC) Code which has been developed by the Bureau of the Census and is widely used to identify and define markets. Theo-

retically, markets are easily defined with the
help of a particular type of price elasticity of
demand, specifically cross-price elasticity. The
term elasticity (η) refers to the measure of
responsiveness of quantity demanded of a product
given a change in that product's price (ceteris
paribus). Cross-price elasticity of demand (η_{xy})
refers to the degree of responsiveness in demand
of a product given a change in the price of
another product (ceteris paribus). If we consider
two goods, X and Y, then η_{xy} ($\eta_{xy} = \%\Delta Qx/\%\Delta Py$) indicates whether they are competing products. If
$\eta_{xy} > 0$, the goods are considered substitutes as
the percentage increase in the price of Y brings
a proportional increase in the quantity of X purchased (X is substituted for Y as Y's price increases). However, this theory is very difficult
to apply. It assumes that all other variables
which affect the quantity of X purchased remain
constant as the price of Y changes. This would
only hold in situations where incomes, tastes and
preferences, and prices of other goods remain constant. Because of the difficulty associated with
using cross-price elasticity, the SIC Code is relied on heavily. This code offers an alternative
set of market definitions. The broadest definition
of a market occurs at the 2-digit level while narrower definitions are made at the 3-, 4-, 5-, and
7-digit levels respectively. For example, SIC Code
20 is a 2-digit major product group which encom-
passes food and kindred products. A 4-digit industry code, say 2011, comprises meat packing while
the 5-digit code 20111 corresponds to fresh beef.
The 7-digit product class is the narrowest. Following my example, this could be 20111-12, whole
carcass beef. The appropriate definition of a market depends on the type of analysis being done.
For instance, if one wants to know how many competitors a firm has for a specific product, then,
one of the narrower definitions would best suit
the need. Alternatively, if the interest is in how
many firms are engaged in food production in general, a broad definition would be better. It should
be noted that the SIC Code does not identify markets solely on the basis of consumer product substitutability. Indeed, the definitions try to incorporate producer substitutability as well. For
instance, the "SIC Code 2711 includes the manufac-

turing of not only passenger cars, but also semi-
trailer trucks and buses."[3]

To begin, one must look at the evolutionary
change that has occurred in the number of product
categories in which these firms operate. Table 3.1
shows that there is an ever increasing degree of
participation in each of the product-industry categories. From 1960 to 1977, participation at the
2-digit level more than doubled. This would indicate that these firms were seeking to diversify
into quite unrelated markets since the number of
2-digit groups served doubled over this period
while 3- and 4-digit group/industry participation
did not.

TABLE 3.1

Mean Number of Product Categories Operated
in by the 200 Firms During 1960,
1965, 1968 and 1977[*]

Product Category	Mean Number of Product Categories			
	1960	1965	1968	1977
4-Digit Industries	13	16	20	21
3-Digit Product Groups	9	11	14	16
2-Digit Major Project Groups	4	5	6	9

[*]Size rank determined according to assets.
SOURCES: Fortune Plant and Product Directories,
1968, and Author's data.

Table 3.2 breaks down the 1977 data by firm
size. It demonstrates the effect on the mean number of product categories operated in as the
smaller firms of the 200 are considered. The mean
falls slowly but continuously for all three categories. As more of the relatively smaller firms
are included, the mean number of product-groups
industries for the whole declines. The mean has its
lowest value in all three categories when all 200
firms are included. Thus the larger firms of the
200, on average, tend to be more diversified regardless of whether a broad or narrow definition
is used.

If one compares the 10 largest with the 200
largest firms in each of the three categories, the
percentage decline in average number of categories
is 12.5% for 2-digit major product groups, 11.1%

TABLE 3.2

Mean Number of Product Categories Operated in
by Asset Size Distribution, 1977

Firms	Mean Number of 4-Digit Industries	Mean Number of 3-Digit Product Groups	Mean Number of 2-Digit Major Product Groups
Largest 10	24	18	12
Largest 20	25	20	13
Largest 30	24	19	13
Largest 40	26	20	12
Largest 50	25	19	12
Largest 60	25	19	12
Largest 70	24	19	11
Largest 80	23	18	11
Largest 90	24	18	11
Largest 100	23	17	10
Largest 110	23	17	10
Largest 120	23	17	10
Largest 130	23	17	10
Largest 140	22	17	10
Largest 150	22	16	10
Largest 160	21	16	10
Largest 170	21	16	9
Largest 180	21	16	9
Largest 190	21	16	9
Largest 200	21	16	9

for 3-digit product groups, and 25% for 4-digit industries. It is apparent that the smaller firms tend to diversify within fewer 2-digit major product groups. This implies that the larger the firm, on average, the more broadly based it is in terms of the number of 2-digit major product groups that it serves.

Table 3.3 indicates the nature of the diversification that has taken place between 1960 and 1977 and shows a clear increase in the degree of diversification at most levels. Looking at the 2-digit group, only 62 of the largest 200 firms participated in more than five different categories in 1960. By 1977 this figure had increased to 152-- a 145% increase. In addition, the number of firms in more than ten 2-digit major product groups rose from 7 in 1960 to 62 in 1977, a 9-fold increase in 17 years. Seven of these firms were active in more than twenty 2-digit groups in 1977, whereas none were active prior to this.

TABLE 3.3

Distribution of 200 Largest Manufacturing Firms
According to the Number of 2-, 3- and 4-Digit
Product Categories Operated in During
1960, 1965, 1968, and 1977

Number of Firms

Number of Product Categories	2-Digit Major Product Group			
	1960	1965	1968	1977
Over 5	62	80	112	152
Over 10	7	14	32	62
Over 20	--	--	--	7
Over 30	--	--	--	1
Over 40	--	--	--	--
Over 50	--	--	--	--

	3-Digit Product Groups			
	1960	1965	1968	1977
Over 5	129	143	122	180
Over 10	56	89	118	134
Over 20	13	24	42	42
Over 30	4	8	13	12
Over 40	--	3	4	3
Over 50	--	--	1	1

	4-Digit Industries			
	1960	1965	1968	1977
Over 5	143	162	184	192
Over 10	91	120	146	160
Over 20	31	47	76	78
Over 30	12	23	39	31
Over 40	5	10	20	15
Over 50	3	5	9	4

SOURCES: Fortune Plant and Product Directories,
1968, and author's data.

Looking at the 3-digit group, there has been an
increase in the "over five" category. In 1960, 129
firms were active in more than five 3-digit groups
and, by 1977, that figure had increased to 180.
Thus, as of 1977, all but twenty of the largest
200 firms served more than five 3-digit groups.
There was a similar increase in the "over ten"
category, but that is the upper limit of the increases. From the "over twenty" category and above
there has been no noticeable increase from 1968 to

1977 even though there were steady increases prior
to that. One possible explanation is that there
may be a tendency for the conglomerate firm to
confine itself to a range of industries, say
twenty-five to thirty, and focus all efforts there.
The data indicate sharp declines in frequency in
the "over thirty" categories for all years shown.
Thus there may be an optimal upper limit of diversification in the 3-digit group.

Regarding the 4-digit industries, virtually
every firm (192 out of 200) produced in more than
five industries in 1977. This figure is up from
184 in 1968 and has continuously increased throughout the years shown. There can be little doubt that
the 200 largest firms have continued to pursue
diversification over a period of time. Only 8 of
these firms are producing in the "five or less"
category. These increases hold in the "over ten"
and "over twenty" categories with approximately
40% (78) of the firms operating more than 4-digit
markets. However, as was true in the 3-digit group,
there is a decline beginning with the "over thirty"
category.

The aggregate picture shows that there have
been sharp increases in the number of product categories that the largest 200 firms served during
the 17 year span 1960-1977, with a slight decline
at the upper levels in 1977. This data indicates
that most of the largest 200 firms are diversified
into more than five 2-digit product groups, more
than ten 3-digit product groups and more than ten
4-digit industries. The number of firms in each of
these groups is steadily increasing. The fact that
192 out of the 200 firms were in more than five
4-digit industries serves to emphasize how diversified these firms have become.

The actual diversification for 1977 can be seen
in Table 3.4. This table shows that 40 of the
largest 200 firms operated in ten or fewer 4-digit
industries in 1977. The highest frequency of firms,
82, was associated with the interval 11-20. Forty-
eight firms operated in the 21-30 interval. In the
intervals above thirty, as was also seen in Table
3.3, the number of firms falls off sharply. Fully
169 of the firms operate in fewer than thirty 4-
digit industries but more than 129 (82 + 47) operate in more than ten. This supports the data in
Tables 3.1 and 3.2, namely, that in 1977 the 200

TABLE 3.4

Frequency Distribution Showing the Multiproduct
Nature of the 200 Largest Manufacturing
Firms, 1977

Number of 4-Digit Industries Served	Number of Firms
1-10	40
11-20	82
21-30	49
31-40	16
41-50	11
51-60	2
61-70	0
71-80	0
81-90	0
91-100	0
101-110	1
	200

largest firms operated, on average, in twenty-one
different 4-digit markets.

Because the economy is dynamic in nature, new
markets are always being opened. Technology, knowledge, and "know how," play a large role in determining these new markets. For instance, technological breakthroughs in motors brought about demand
for oil and oil related products while scientific
discoveries about oil opened up markets in chemicals. Advances in the science of electronics led
to the invention of the computer. Since there is
a diversity of markets in the economy, the question that arises is whether the largest manufacturing firms are diversifying such that they now
compete in many of these same markets. The set of
tables, 3.5-3.10, below, taken together, are designed to indicate whether a web of markets does
exist as a result of the diversification efforts
of these firms.

Table 3.5 presents the frequency distribution
for the primary 4-digit industries of 102 of the
200 firms. Of the 98 firms not included in this
table, 40 collectively named 20 different product
markets as their primary market. The remaining 58
were spread over 58 different product markets. As
Table 3.5 indicates, 21 or just over 10% of the
largest 200 firms were primarily engaged in the
production of petroleum refining products. This is

TABLE 3.5

Frequency Distribution of 4-Digit Industries
Listed as the Primary Industry for 102 of
the 200 Largest Manufacturing Firms, 1977

4-Digit Industry	Description	Number of Firms
1311	Crude oil and natural gas	4
3312	Steel works	11
2834	Pharmaceutical preparations	9
3573	Computers	7
3714	Motor vehicle equipment	7
3711	Motor vehicles	6
2818	Industrial organic chemicals (NEC)*	5
3011	Tires and inner tubes	5
2821	Plastics and resins	4
2844	Soaps, detergents, cosmetics and toilet prep.	4
2911	Petroleum refining	21
3721	Aircraft and parts	4
1925	Guided missiles and space vehicles	3
2011	Meat packing plants	3
2111	Cigarettes	3
2621	Paper mills	3
3861	Photographic equipment	3

102 of the larg-
est firms

*NEC--not elsewhere classified

almost double the next highest number of firms,
11, primarily engaged in the production of steel.
It is obvious that the number of firms in each 4-
digit industry drops off rather sharply after the
crude oil and natural gas category.

One attempt to measure the extent to which
these 200 firms face each other in a web of markets involves a tabulation procedure devised by
the Bureau of the Census. The bureau's methodology
is to compute the difference between the number of
these firms primarily engaged in a particular (2-
digit) major industry group and the total number
of firms operating in that group (this difference,
is designated as secondary activity in that group).
A large difference, relatively speaking, would
imply the existence of frequent encounters between

these firms. Table 3.6 gives the results of a study
done by the Census Bureau in 1963.

To facilitate comparison, indicating the degree
of secondary activity that exists in each of the
major industry groups, ratios have been computed.
These ratios are shown in the last column of Table
3.6. The greatest secondary activity was found in
the rubber and plastic products group which had a
ratio of 1.0:16.2. This means that there were 16.2
times as many firms with plants in rubber and
plastics products as there were firms primarily
engaged in the production of these goods. So, although only four firms listed this as their primary product group, the presence of sixty-five
firms indicates a significant frequency of encoun-
ter in that group. The second highest ratio, 1.0:
12.6 occurred in the instruments and miscellaneous
products group. This group includes such products
as professional instruments, optical goods, clocks,
jewelry, toys, amusements, and pens. There were
12.6 times as many firms producing these products
as were primarily engaged in their production. The
smallest ratio, 1.0:1.0 was found in the tobacco
products group. Here, there is no secondary activity at all. That is, all firms involved in the production of tobacco products were primarily involved
in that major industry group.

If we compute a simple mean of these ratios for
1963, it is approximately 1.0:6.0. This means that
every major industry group had, on average, six
times as many firms with plants in that group as
the number of firms primarily engaged therein.

For comparison purposes, Table 3.7 applies the
Bureau's methodology to the 1977 data. It is
apparent that between 1963 and 1977 the degree of
interaction had changed dramatically. First, the
highest ratio, 1.0:32.0, was considerably higher
than its counterpart 1.0:16.2. Also, this highest
degree of secondary activity occurred in the tex-
tile and leather products group instead of in the
rubber and plastics group. Three additional major
product groups, instruments, printing and publishing, and furniture and fixtures, had ratios higher
than the highest in 1963. The lowest ratio, 1.0:
1.3, again occurred in the tobacco products group,
but even here there had been some increase in
activity.

During the fourteen-year period, 1963-1977, the
mean ratio had increased to 1.0:10.7 which means,

TABLE 3.6

Two Hundred Largest Manufacturing Companies: Comparison Between Companies
Primarily Engaged in and Companies with Plants
in Major Industry Groups, 1963

Number of Companies among 200 Largest

Major Industry Group	(a) Primarily Engaged in-	(b) With Plants in-	Difference (b-a)	Ratio (a:b)
Food and kindred products	29	48	19	1.0: 1.6
Tobacco products	6	6	0	1.0: 1.0
Textile and leather products	4	27	23	1.0: 6.7
Apparel and related products	0	12	12	
Furniture and fixtures	0	12	12	
Paper and lumber products	12	83	71	1.0: 6.9
Printing and publishing	6	48	42	1.0: 8.0
Chemicals and allied products	31	101	70	1.0: 3.3
Petroleum and coal products	10	20	10	1.0: 2.0
Rubber and plastics products	4	65	61	1.0:16.2
Stone, clay, and glass products	8	46	38	1.0: 5.7
Primary metals industries	18	62	44	1.0: 3.4
Fabricated metal products	6	70	64	1.0:11.6
Nonelectrical machinery	12	76	64	1.0: 6.3
Electrical machinery	19	59	40	1.0: 3.1
Transportation equipment	30	53	23	1.0: 1.8
Instruments, miscellaneous products	5	63	58	1.0:12.6

NOTE: To prevent disclosure of the operations of individual companies the Census
Bureau combined lumber and allied products with paper and paper products. For the
same reason instruments were combined with miscellaneous products.

SOURCE: Concentration Ratios in Manufacturing Industry, 1963 pt. 2, tables 23,
24, prepared for the Subcommittee on Antitrust and Monopoly 1967.

TABLE 3.7

Two Hundred Largest Manufacturing Companies: Comparison Between Companies
Primarily Engaged in and Companies with Plants
in Major Industry Groups, 1977

Number of Companies Among 200 Largest

Major Industry Group	(a) Primarily Engaged in-	(b) With Plants in-	Difference (b-a)	Ratio (a:b)
Food and kindred products	20	58	38	1.0: 2.9
Tobacco products	3	4	1	1.0: 1.3
Textile and leather products	1	32	31	1.0:32.0
Apparel and related products	0	18	18	
Furniture and fixtures	3	50	47	1.0:16.6
Paper and lumber products	6	47	41	1.0: 7.8
Printing and publishing	1	23	22	1.0:23.0
Chemicals and allied products	33	115	82	1.0: 3.4
Petroleum and coal	5	41	36	1.0: 8.2
Rubber and plastics products	6	58	52	1.0: 9.6
Stone, clay and glass products	5	47	42	1.0: 9.4
Primary metals industries	17	64	47	1.0: 3.7
Fabricated metal products	5	77	72	1.0:15.4
Nonelectrical machinery	15	95	80	1.0: 6.3
Electrical machinery	14	84	70	1.0: 6.0
Transportation equipment	22	62	40	1.0: 2.8
Instruments, miscellaneous products	4	94	90	1.0:23.5

on average, there were 10.7 times as many firms
operating in each group as the firms that primarily
produced in that group. This is an increase of 78%.
Clearly the structure of the manufacturing sector
is such that the 200 largest firms had encountered
each other in several markets in the past and are
continuously increasing the number of these encounters through their diversification efforts.

Another technique that may be used to measure
the degree of interaction between the 200 firms
measures their frequency of activity in particular
markets. Table 3.8 shows the 2-digit major product
groups having the highest frequency of firms. As
the table indicates, the chemical and allied products market is the most popular, being served by
115 firms. This means that 57.5% of the 200 firms
have plants which produce in this major product
group. The group, machinery except electrical, has
the second largest number of firms, 95, while the
electrical equipment and supplies group has 84.
Whereas these three product groups are traditionally popular with manufacturing firms, the next
group, wholesale trade, is not. The appearance of
wholesale trade and of real estate on this list is
noteworthy. The fact that 37 manufacturing firms
are involved in real estate means that a group of
these firms are diversifying along broad lines.

The same kind of analysis can be made if 3-digit
product groups are used. Table 3.9 shows the groups
more frequented by the 200 firms. Again, chemicals
includes the largest number of firms, 75, followed
by plastics (also in major product group 28), with
60. The third and fourth places are filled by two
nontraditional groups 738, miscellaneous business
services, and 509, miscellaneous wholesales. That
these two product groups are served by so many
firms again indicates the broad degree of diversification that some of the large manufacturing firms
have attained.

It should be noted that as the focus changes
from the 2-digit major product groups to the 3-
digit product groups and, finally, to the 4-digit
industries, the market definition is narrowing.
Thus, we are moving from broad rather encompassing
definitions of markets, to narrow, very specific
definitions. It is to be expected that the number
of firms in any market will fall as this narrowing
occurs. Even so, there are 75 firms engaged in

TABLE 3.8

Two-Digit Major Product Groups With the
Highest Occurrence of the 200 Largest
Manufacturing Firms, 1977

2-Digit Major Product Group	Description	Number of Firms
28	Chemical and Allied Pro- ducts	115
35	Machinery, Except Elec- trical	95
36	Electrical Equipment and Supplies	84
50	Wholesale Trade	82
34	Fabricated Metal Products	77
33	Primary Metals Industries	64
73	Miscellaneous Business Services	63
37	Transportation Equipment	62
38	Instruments and Related/ Products	60
20	Food and Kindred/Products	58
30	Rubber and Plastic Pro- ducts, NEC	58
13	Oil and Gas Extraction	54
32	Stone, Clay and Glass Products	47
26	Paper and Allied Products	47
29	Petroleum Refining	41
12	Bituminous Coal and Lig- nite Mining	40
65	Real Estate	37
14	Nonmetallic Minerals, Except Fuels	37
39	Miscellaneous Manufactur- ing Industries	34
22	Textile Mill Products	32

product group 281, or 38% of the 200 firms, quite
a substantial percentage for a more narrowly defined market.

Table 3.10 lists the 4-digit industries which
are most frequently served by the largest manufacturing firms. Just as in the analyses of the 3-
digit product groups and the 2-digit major product
groups, the highest frequency occurs in major product group 28, chemical and allied products. Specifically, industries 2821, plastics materials;

TABLE 3.9

Three-Digit Product Groups With the Highest
Occurrence of the 200 Largest
Manufacturing Firms, 1977

3-Digit Product Group	Description	Number of Firms
281	Industrial Chemicals	75
282	Plastic Materials and Synthetics	60
739	Miscellaneous Business Services	60
289	Miscellaneous Chemical Products	46
131	Crude Petroleum and Natural Gas	42
307	Miscellaneous Plastic Products	41
121	Bituminous Coal and Lignite Mining	40
371	Motor Vehicles and Equipment	39
287	Agricultural Chemicals	38
349	Miscellaneous Fabricated Metal Products	38
284	Soap, Cleaners and Toilet Goods	37
353	Construction and Related Machinery	37
344	Fabricated Structural Metal Products	36
356	General Industrial Machinery	36
366	Communications Equipment	35
264	Miscellaneous Converted Paper Products	34
331	Blast Furnace and Basic Steel Products	33
204	Grain Mill Products	32
367	Electronic Components and Accessories	32
335	Nonferrows Rolling and Drawing	31
354	Metal Working Machinery	31
362	Electrical Industrial Apparatus	31
283	Drugs	30
329	Miscellaneous Nonmetallic Mineral Products	29
384	Medical Instruments and Supplies	29
372	Aircraft and Parts	29

TABLE 3.10

Four-Digit Industries With the Highest Occurrence
of the 200 Largest Manufacturing Firms, 1977

4-Digit Industry	Description	Number of Firms
2821	Plastic Materials	57
2818	Industrial Organic Chemicals (NEC)	55
2819	Industrial Inorganic Chemicals (NEC)	54
3079	Miscellaneous Plastic Products	47
1311	Crude Petroleum and Natural Gas	42
3662	Radio and TV Communications Equipment	38
3714	Motor Vehicle Parts and Accessories	37
1211	Coal	36
2899	Chemicals and Chemical Preparations (NEC)	33
2911	Petroleum Refining	32
3069	Fabricated Rubber Products	30
2042	Prepared Feeds for Animals and Fowls	27
3312	Blast Furnaces and Steel Mills	25
7392	Business Consulting Services	25
2879	Agricultural Chemicals (NEC)	24
3679	Electronic Components (NEC)	23
2621	Paper Mills, Except bldg. Paper	23
3531	Construction Machinery	22
3634	Electric Housewares and Fans	22
3841	Surgical and Medical Instruments	22
4411	Deep Sea Foreign Transportation	22
5541	Gasoline Service Stations	22
0811	Timber Tracts	21
2421	Sawmills and Planing Mills	21
2871	Fertilizers	21
4612	Crude Petroleum Pipelines	21
3589	Service Industry Machines (NEC)	21
3494	Valves and Pipe Fittings	21
3443	Fabricated Plate Work	20
8911	Engineering and Architectural Services	20

2818, industrial organic chemicals, NEC; and 2819,
industrial inorganic chemicals, NEC, rank first,
second, and third respectively. Fifty-seven, or
29% of the largest 200 firms, are engaged in the

production of chemicals or plastics while 21% are
engaged in the production of crude petroleum and
natural gas. These five industries with the highest frequency of firms are related through vertical contact points. Oil, of course, is a major
input used in the production of all types of chemicals and plastics. Thus, at the narrow, 4-digit
industry level, not only do the firms frequently
meet one another in the various markets of the
economy, but there are also strong vertical links
between them. These Tables, 3.8-3.10, lend further
support to the thesis that a web of markets exists
in the manufacturing sector of the economy.

Having noted the nature of the diversification
exhibited by the largest manufacturing firms in
the economy, one must determine exactly which of
these firms have achieved the highest degree of
diversification. Table 3.11 lists twenty-five
firms that actively sought acquisitions during the
period 1961-1974. Since the data from chapter 1
indicates that most mergers occurring in this
period were the conglomerate type, these firms
should be among the most diversified in 1977. The
phrase "most diversified," however, is not easily
defined.

As has been stated previously, to diversify, in
this case, generally means to bring together unlike products into a firm. At first it does not
seem that there should be an difficulty in identifying unlike products; however, measuring degrees
of diversification is complicated. There are several alternative definitions that could be used
and each may bring different results as to how
diversified a particular firm is.

A measure of diversification could be made by
using a Herfindahl Index. The Herfindahl Index is
defined:

$$\underline{D} = 1 - \sum_{\underline{i} = 1}^{n} \underline{P}_{\underline{i}}^{2}$$

Here $\underline{D}$ stands for diversification, $\underline{n}$ for the number of product categories (industries), and $\underline{P}_{i}$ for
the ratio of sales in the $\underline{n}$th category (industry)
to total sales. This index describes the arrangement of a firm's activity. "Diversification is
zero when a firm is active in a single industry
and approaches unity when the firm in question

TABLE 3.11

Twenty-five Large Corporations Making Extensive Acquisitions, 1961-1974

Corporation	Sales[a] 1974 ($)	Sales[a] 1960 ($)	Growth, 1960-1974 (Percentage)	Rank Among Industrials 1974	Rank Among Industrials 1960
ITT	11,154	811	1,375	10	51
Continental Oil	7,041	694	1,015	17	64
Atlantic-Richfield	6,740	561	1,201	18	77
Occidental Oil	5,719	3	--	20	--[b]
Tenneco	5,001	535	935	25	85
Phillips Petroleum	4,981	1,200	415	25	31
LTV	4,768	148	3,222	29	285
RCA	4,594	1,486	209	31	25
Union Oil	4,419	427	1,035	34	107
Rockwell Industries	4,408	116	3,800	35	353
Sun Oil	3,800	750	507	37	59
Beatrice Foods	3,541	443	799	42	105
W. R. Grace	3,472	553	629	44	80
Greyhound	3,458	287	1,205	45	--[c]
Litton Industries	3,082	188	1,639	53	249
McDonald-Douglas	3,075	437	604	54	110
Ralston Purina	3,073	510	603	55	92
Philip Morris	3,042	330	922	57	140
Singer	2,661	526	506	66	86
CPC International	2,570	276	831	71	171
TRW	2,486	420	592	76	113
Georgia Pacific	2,432	222	1,095	79	213
Gulf and Western	2,296	24	--	83	--[d]
Textron	2,114	383	552	89	124
FMC	2,074	364	570	91	129
Total 25 Corporations	102,001	11,694	772		
All Manufacturers	1,010,000	431,329	134		

[a] Sales for consolidated subsidiaries.
[b] Not among the 1000 largest industrials in 1960.
[c] Rank based on predecessor corporation.
[d] Not primarily an industrial corporation in 1960.

SOURCE: Willard F. Mueller, "Conglomerates: A "Nonindustry," in Walter Adams, The Structure of American Industry, 5th ed. (New York: Macmillan, 1977), p. 446.

produces equally in a large number of different
industries."[4] This approach to measuring diversification was taken by Charles Berry and others.
Unfortunately, the data necessary for computing
the Herfindahl Index is not available in the 10-K
Reports. The SEC does not require that sales be
reported for anything other than broad product
lines. Most firms include several 2-digit groups
within one broad classification. Others do not.
There is no rhyme, reason, or consistency to this
information. Therefore, without access to confi-
dential financial data, the Index cannot be computed.[5]

Another possible definition views diversification in terms of the number of 4-digit markets in
which a firm has operations, the argument being
that a narrow definition yields the actual number
of markets a firm faces and thus is the appropriate measure for diversification. There are problems associated with using a 4-digit definition
since there are several 4-digit markets within
most 3-digit groupings and in all 2-digit groupings. It is conceivable that a firm could be
highly diversified by 4-digit criteria but really
not produce products outside of a particular 2-
digit product group or a couple of 2-digit groups.
Can one say that a firm operating in many 4-digit
industries, but within one or two 2-digit groups,
is a diversified firm? The answer obviously is yes
if you use a 4-digit criterion.[6]

This raises some doubts concerning a firm's
position as a conglomerate. A conglomerate produces many products, all of which are unrelated.
With regards to market classification, then, the
degree of diversity here would have to be more
toward a measure of how many 2-digit markets a
firm faces, not the number of 4-digit markets. By
using a 2-digit definition, one is concerned with
the breadth of the contact points in the economy
that a firm has, not the number of narrowly defined markets in which it operates.

Finally, the definition could rest on a 3-digit
classification. Here we have neither the problem
of breadth that is lacking in a 4-digit definition,
nor the narrowness that is lacking in a 2-digit
definition. This seems to be an appealing compromise. However, even though it tends to blend together the two extremes, a 3-digit definition is
not necessarily correct. A compromise definition

does not necessarily resolve the criticisms leveled against the other definitions. Although each of the three definitions has strong as well as weak attributes, identification of the most diversified firms, according to all three definitions, might be possible.

Using a 2-digit definition, Table 3.12 lists the thirty-one most diversified firms (of the largest 200) and the number of product groups they serve. Of the thirty-one firms, only nine were shown in Table 3.11. This means that when a 2-digit definition is used, only nine of the twenty-five firms in Table 3.11 appear to have made acquisitions that were wholly unrelated to each other.

Table 3.13 includes those firms that were found to be the most diversified when a 3-digit definition is used. Seven firms in this table are also included in Table 3.11. Finally, Table 3.14 contains the thirty-two most diversified firms when a 4-digit industry criterion is used. Regarding those firms making extensive acquisitions, nine appear in Table 3.14. Apparently only a small number of the firms making acquisitions between 1961 and 1974 have become quite diversified as few of the firms identified in Tables 3.13-3.15 are those contained in Table 3.12.

Is there a common set of firms included in all three tables? Do some firms consistently fit the description of being diversified, regardless of the criterion used? Table 3.15 lists eighteen such firms, each of which is unmistakenly a conglomerate. It is interesting to note that Gulf and Western headed the list of firms in all three Tables, 3.12-3.14.

Alternatively, instead of considering the most diversified firms to be those meeting the criteria of Table 3.15, one could argue that the appropriate qualification could be either definition. In this sense, any firm which is included in either Table, 3.12, 3.13, or 3.14 could be considered within the group of firms exhibiting the greatest diversity. Forty-four such firms are found and are listed in Table 3.16.

The Spearman Rank Correlation Coefficient, which measures the strength of tendency for a firm ranked by a particular definition to retain that ranking when a different definition is used can be used to test whether the different definitions

TABLE 3.12

Firms Exhibiting the Greatest Diversity in Terms
of 2-Digit Industries Served, 1977

Name	Number of 2-Digit Groups	Rank by Assets
Gulf and Western	31	37
ITT	23	11
Mobil	23	3
W. R. Grace	22	53
Jim Walter	22	121
Signal Co.	21	81
Ogden	21	189
Beatrice Foods	19	83
Bethlehem Steel	18	28
Westinghouse	18	25
North American Phillips	16	183
Greyhound	16	125
Ashland Oil	16	64
Getty Oil	16	36
General Electric	16	9
U. S. Steel	16	13
Tenneco	16	15
Sun Co.	16	26
Williams Companies	15	98
Teledyne	15	142
Consolidated Foods	15	161
Continental Group	15	60
Goodyear Tire and Rubber	15	30
Dow Chemical	14	17
Union Oil of California	14	29
RCA	14	32
United Technologies	14	52
Armco Steel	14	55
Kerr-McGee	14	101
Bendix	14	103
General Tire and Rubber Co.	14	124

yield significantly different ranking for the
forty-four firms in this set; and since it can
take on values between plus and minus one, it is
evident, that each of the extremes indicates strong
positive or negative rank correlation.[7]

The forty-four firms were ranked by 2-, 3-, and
4-digit definitions and coefficients were derived
for each combination of two. All coefficients computed
were significant at the 0.01 level. In the
2-digit and 3-digit pairing, the coefficient was

TABLE 3.13

Firms Exhibiting the Greatest Diversity in Terms
of 3-Digit Industries Served, 1977

Name	Number of 3-Digit Groups	Rank by Assets
Gulf and Western	74	37
Consolidated Foods	43	161
Beatrice Foods	41	83
ITT	38	11
Jim Walter	38	121
Signal	37	81
Mobil	36	3
W. R. Grace	35	53
Ogden	34	189
Textron	32	113
Teledyne	32	142
General Electric	31	9
Westinghouse	30	25
North American Phillips	29	183
Bendix	28	103
American Brands	27	59
3M	27	45
International Paper	27	41
RCA	27	32
Dow Chemical	27	17
Tenneco	26	15
Bethlehem Steel	26	28
Northwest Industries	26	110
U. S. Steel	25	13
United Technologies	25	52
Ashland Oil	25	64
Getty Oil	24	36
I. C. Industries	24	63
Walter Kidde	24	172
Continental Group	24	60

0.55; and for a 2-digit and 4-digit match, it was
0.44. Thus, the tendency for firms ranked by a 2-
digit definition to retain this ranking when a 3-
or 4-digit definition is used is clearly weak,
compared to the coefficient derived for the 3-
digit and 4-digit combination, which was 0.85.
Here the tendency for firms ranked as most diversified by a 3-digit definition to retain that ranking by a 4-digit definition was significantly
positive. These tests demonstrate how potentially
important the definition of diversification (and

TABLE 3.14

Firms Exhibiting the Greatest Diversity in Terms
of 4-Digit Industries Served, 1977

Name	Number of 4-Digit Groups	Rank by Assets
Gulf and Western	105	37
Beatrice Foods	64	83
Consolidated Foods	58	161
Signal Company	52	81
International Paper	48	41
Mobil Oil	46	3
ITT	46	11
Jim Walter	46	121
Ogden	46	189
White Consolidated	46	200
Teledyne	44	142
North American Phillips	42	183
Textron	42	113
W. R. Grace	42	53
RCA	42	32
General Electric	41	9
I. C. Industries	40	63
Dow Chemical	39	17
Westinghouse	39	25
American Brands	37	59
Bendix	35	103
3M	33	45
Northwest Industries	33	110
E. I. du pont	32	19
Bethlehem Steel	32	28
Rockwell International	32	48
Tenneco	31	15
Dresser Industries	31	80
Greyhound	31	125
Mead	31	146
Walter Kidde	31	172
Alleghany Ludlum	31	178

of a conglomerate) can be. Those firms that are active in a broad array of product groups are not the same firms that are active in many narrower subsets of the economy.

One other bit of information can be gathered from these forty-four firms. They can be grouped according to asset size to see if high diversification is more or less a function of size. The most diversified firms represented here include

TABLE 3.15

Firms Exhibiting the Greatest Diversity
By 2-, 3-, and 4-Digit Definition, 1977

Name	Ranked by Assets
Gulf and Western	37
ITT	11
Mobil	3
W. R. Grace	53
Jim Walter	121
Signal Corp.	81
Ogden	189
Beatrice	83
Bethlehem Steel	28
Westinghouse	25
North American Phillips	183
General Electric	9
Tenneco	15
Teledyne	142
Consolidated Foods	161
Dow Chemical	17
RCA	32
Bendix	103

virtually all sizes from the largest to the smallest. But when looking at Table 3.17, one sees that there is a positive relationship between firm size and degree of diversification. A way to evaluate Table 3.17 is to consider the probability that one of the forty-four firms chosen at random is one of the very largest firms (Asset Rank 1-50). This probability is 0.41 (18/44). Thus, it is almost a one in two chance that the firm chosen will be among the very largest. At the other end of the spectrum, asset rank 151-200, the probability that a firm chosen at random from the forty-four would be from this rank is 0.14 (6/44), obviously a much lower probability.

Another approach is to consider the probability that a firm chosen at random from either of the four categories would be among the most diversified. If one chose a firm among the largest fifty, the probability would be 0.36 (18/50) that it also would be one of the most diversified firms. This probability falls consistently from the largest asset category to the smallest. In the final category, 151-200, the probability that one of these fifty firms is also one of the most diversified is

TABLE 3.16

Firms Exhibiting the Greatest Diversity by Either
2-, 3-, or 4-Digit Definition, 1977

Name	Rank by Assets
Gulf	37
Beatrice Foods	83
Consolidated Foods	161
Signal Corp.	81
Mobil Oil	3
ITT	11
Jim Walter	121
Ogden	189
Teledyne	142
North American Phillips	183
W. R. Grace	53
RCA	32
General Electric	9
Dow Chemical	17
Westinghouse	25
Bendix	103
Tenneco	15
Bethlehem Steel	28
Ashland Oil	64
Getty Oil	36
U. S. Steel	13
Continental Group	60
United Technologies	52
Textron	113
American Brands	59
3M	45
International Paper	41
Northwest Industries	110
I. C. Industries	63
Walter Kidde	172
Greyhound	125
Sun	26
Goodyear	30
Union Oil	29
Armco	55
Kerr-McGee	101
General Tire	124
Williams	98
White Consolidated	200
E. I. du pont	19
Dresser Industries	80
Mead	146
Rockwell International	48
Allegheny Ludlum	178

TABLE 3.17

Asset Rank of the Forty-four
Most Diversified Firms, 1977

Category of Asset Rank	Number of Firms
1-50	18
51-100	11
101-150	9
151-200	6
Total	44

0.12 (6/50). Table 3.17 and these probabilities tell us that the larger the firm, the more likely it is to be among the most diversified.

It is difficult to state with certainty that a web of markets is actually present in the manufacturing sector of the economy. Over half of the firms studied are involved in major product group 28, chemical and allied products; and slightly less than half are involved in major product groups 35, machinery, except electrical, and 36, electrical equipment and supplies. Considering this, and the high degree of participation by many of these firms at the 3- and 4-digit levels of these major product groups, it is evident that many of these firms face each other frequently in a set of unrelated markets. Evidence was also obtained which demonstrated a high frequency of vertical as well as horizontal contact points.

Table 3.16 revealed a set of eighteen of the most diversified firms, each described as diversified regardless of whether a broad or narrow definition is used. Gulf and Western was the most diversified by each definition. When the Spearman Rank Correlation Coefficient was used to compare the results of using alternative definitions of diversification, it became evident that the 2-digit definition ranked firms significantly different than did the 3- and 4-digit definitions. Thus the choice of definition is quite crucial in identifying those firms considered most diversified.

4 Conglomerate Firms and Labor Unions

LABOR UNIONS pervade the industrial sector of the economy. Lloyd Reynolds has pointed out that "a substantial majority (of wage earners) are (union) members (in manufacturing), although the ratio varies in different branches of manufacturing-- high in steel and automobiles, low in textiles."[1] To evaluate the response of labor unions to the emergence of conglomerate firms in the manufacturing sector of the economy, one needs to analyze the impact of firm diversification on the collective bargaining relationship and discuss labor's adjustment to this new condition in the marketplace. The effect of conglomerates on unions has a broader significance as well, for any substantial change in the structure of the economy will affect the degree of competition that exists between firms. Also, capitalism, as we know it, may be permanently changed.

Sydney and Beatrice Webb defined a trade union as a continuous association of wage earners existing for the purpose of maintaining or improving the working lives of the laboring class.[2] As competition forced the entrepreneur to reduce his cost in order to survive and make a profit, these reductions took the form of low wages and undesirable working conditions. Individually, each worker realized that he was not in a position to influence his employer to raise his wage or improve his conditions of work. The employer was faced with enough pressure on profits without additional pressure from labor; if one laborer demanded more, he probably would lose his job. The cost to the employer of losing this individual was less than

the cost of raising wages and losing profits. From
the individual's viewpoint, the cost of losing his
job was great indeed. Thus he stood to lose by
demanding more from his employer.

The situation is different, however, if collective action is taken by workers, for if all workers quit (strike), then the cost to the employer
is great. Workers, recognizing this difference,
began to organize in the United States at the
beginning of the nineteenth century for the purpose of improving wages and working conditions,
the like of which could not be achieved by individual action.

One precept in collective bargaining is that in
order for a union of workers to obtain their demands they must have bargaining power of at least
equal magnitude to that of the employer. Bargaining power refers to the ability of one party in
the negotiating process to cause the other party
to reach an agreement on its terms. A union without bargaining power, or with eroding power, will
not be able to maintain or improve the wages and/
or working conditions of its membership.

Bargaining power is obtained in part from the
economic variables, and from the tactics and
strategies used by the negotiators during the bargaining process. Those economic variables which
affect power are the elasticity of demand for
labor (the responsiveness of the quantity demanded
of labor given a change in labor's wage rate) in
the firm/industry, the profitability of the firm/
industry, and the ratio of labor costs to total
costs in the production process of the firm/
industry. When a firm has inelastic (less responsive) demand for labor, the tendency is less for
it to lay off workers when wages rise. Conversely,
the more elastic (more responsive) is the firm's
demand, the more likely it will substitute other
inputs for labor when wages rise. Therefore, the
union's bargaining power over wages is strongest
when the demand for labor is inelastic.

Profits also influence the degree of bargaining
power that accrues to each party in the bargaining
process. The higher the rate of profits, the
greater the ability of the firm to pay for higher
wages and/or better working conditions. Union
negotiators are more confident in making demands
when they know the firm can afford "reasonable"

increases in wages. Finally, unions will not have
the same bargaining power when labor costs account
for a large proportion of total costs as they
might if labor costs comprise only a small fraction of total costs, for even a small increase in
labor costs becomes a large increase in total
costs.

In addition to the negotiators' power and the
power obtained from economic variables, organization, which is the composition of the groups represented on the two sides of the bargaining table,
also determines bargaining power. The constituency
of these groups will affect the balance of power
in negotiating. Firm diversification necessarily
affects bargaining structure.

If the weight of influence carried by the two
parties to the negotiation are not similar, then
there is an imbalance of power in the bargaining
structure. For instance, imagine a bargaining
structure where a single-product firm faces a
union representing a set of its employees. If
these employees were crucial to the production
process, then the union would bring equal power to
the bargaining table because either side could
shut down the production process if an impasse in
negotiations occurred. Or, a bargaining structure
could exist where a multi-product firm faced a
union representing a set of workers crucial to the
production process of one of the firm's subsidiaries. Here there would be unequal power brought
to the bargaining table since, with impasse, the
firm could prohibit all the workers of this union
from working, but the union could not shut down all
the subsidiaries of the multi-product firm. Equal
power requires that each side have the equivalent
impact on the other. For equal power to exist in
this situation, the labor side of the table must
include the unions that are crucial to the production process of all of the firm's subsidiaries.

It follows, then, that conglomerates bring to
the bargaining table a type of power that single-
product firms do not have; that is, diversification gives them a greater ability to handle the
strike threat of a union. There are several elements operating here. Recall that according to
the "deep pockets" theory, a large conglomerate
has great staying power; it has more resources
from which to draw than a smaller, single-product
firm. That being the case, the threat of a strike--

one of the unions' strongest weapons--is not as
menacing to a large conglomerate firm. Perhaps
only one of the conglomerates many product lines
is being threatened. Because it is diversified,
the firm can easily move more resources from one
unit to another (see Appendix A). Diversification
conveys a luxury. The firm has the alternative to
move resources to less problematic plants. This
is not to say that the costs and/or difficulties
associated with such a move are nonexistent,
because no firm, conglomerate or otherwise, wants
to shutdown profitable units. The point is that
the smaller, single-product firm does not have
this option. This ease, afforded because of
diversification, reduces the effect of the strike
and therefore the power of the union.

Galbraith has argued that an imbalance of power
between buyers and sellers of a particular good or
service prompts an attempt by the less powerful to
achieve equal bargaining power. He noted, "power
on one side of the market creates both the need
for, and the prospect of reward to the exercise of
countervailing power from the other side."[3]
Galbraith pointed to unions as the classic example
of countervailing power. "In the ultimate sense it
was the power of the steel industry, not the organizing abilities of John L. Lewis and Phillip
Murray, that brought the United Steel Workers into
being. The economic power that the worker faced in
the sale of his labor . . . made it necessary that
he organize for his own protection."[4]

Countervailing power, Galbraith argues, "is a
self-generating force."[5] What this implies is that
one must expect it to evolve naturally in a market
where an imbalance of power exists. Therefore one
would expect the emergence of conglomerate power
at the bargaining table to beget countervailing
power by the affected unions. George Hildebrand
has pointed out that unions have already undergone changes in structure to offset the power of
conglomerates.

> As with the typical diversified corporation,
> they (unions) often spread well beyond
> established product boundaries. Indeed,
> organizations such as the Automobile Work-
> ers, the Steelworkers, and the Teamsters,
> each led by aggressive and capable men,
> have expanded so far in the past three

decades that they now can be described as
"conglomerate" unions, with all the structural complexity of their large corporate
counterparts.[6]

He further notes that the explanation of this
movement to 'conglomerate' complexity is to "extend the power of their organization. . . . Power
can be increased by organizing the unorganized, by
displacing other unions, by absorbing them, and by
providing leadership to alliances formed with
them."[7] As seen below, unions have chosen to change
the bargaining structure (and thereby reestablish
their bargaining power vis-à-vis conglomerate
firms) by seeking alliances amongst themselves.
Hildebrand points to this as he observes, "the
basic reason for the emergence of the coalition
(alliance) movement is the power of the multi-
plant enterprise today."[8]

Mr. J. P. Molony, vice-president of the United
Steel Workers, in testifying before the Senate
Subcommittee on Antitrust in February, 1970, said
that unions have no choice but to answer the rise
of conglomerate firms with similar structures.
"If the companies we deal with expand into many
product areas, the obvious answer is for unions to
move with them. This we are doing. These efforts
have picked up the descriptive name of "coordinated
bargaining" or . . . "coalition bargaining." Coordinated bargaining is still in its infancy, but
we believe it will be the wave of the future."[9]
He goes on to state that unions have no choice but
to seek structures as large and as diversified as
the large conglomerate.

> Unless somehow each of the separate unions
> with an interest in the conglomerate can
> band together and present a united front of
> coalition or coordinated bargaining to each
> of these conglomerates, then I suggest . . .
> that collective bargaining will break down,
> and, in the process, the carefully built-up
> company or industry standards achieved
> through years of bargaining are threatened
> with serious erosion.[10]

During these hearings, Mr. Brubaker, also a representative of the United Steel Workers, outlined

the disadvantages that a single union encounters when bargaining with a multi-product firm.

Yet, when we come up to some of these other companies where they have them operating in a whole series of different industries, we find that we have one little segment of them in metal working, somebody else has a piece of them over here in chemicals, somebody else has some over in plastics, somebody else has part of the company over in coal mining, they can cut us to pieces, literally.[11]

What Mr. Brubaker refers to when he says "they can cut us to pieces" is the tactic known as divide and conquer. Often a part of this tactic is whip-sawing, which refers to the practice, in this case on the part of management, of evaluating the strength of the various unions and then seeking to reach agreement first with the weakest of these unions. The firm would use the leverage of this agreement to influence its bargaining with the other unions. Unions, of course, may also use this tactic. They would go after the most vulnerable firm in an industry first, then use the leverage from this agreement to wrest concessions from stronger firms. Kenneth Alexander describes the use of this tactic in the following way:

Simply put, conglomeration shifts tactical bargaining and strike power in favor of management. Management can now negotiate from a central position of strength, against separate opponents isolated into the many small fronts of different bargaining units. With tactically-separated opponents, management now has the opportunity to design the grand strategy, to "pick off," to whip-saw, to play one opponent against the other, to time its separate bargaining positions and movements to its own advantage, to temporarily or permanently shift production, etc. Now, use of the strike or strike threat by an opponent is of much lesser consequence within the broad dimensions of the multi-industry firm.[12]

Reynolds notes that where whipsaw tactics are used, there is often a counter tactic. "The obvious reply to whipsawing is counterorganization. This maneuvering and countermaneuvering tends to enlarge the size of the bargaining units."[13] The use of whipsaw tactics by conglomerates has prompted the unions to resort to coordinated/coalition bargaining. Multi-product firms and multi-union alliances represent the enlarged bargaining units predicted by Reynolds.

The diversified nature of a firm is not its only source of unequal bargaining power. Unions argue that there is increased difficulty in obtaining information about a firm once it becomes a conglomerate.

> Conglomerates also present us with an information gap. In order to bargain intelligently with any company, we need to know facts and figures about a company's operations. We need to know the company's profit level, trend of sales and other key economic factors. Under current financial practices, conglomerates lump all of their operations . . . into one consolidated figure.

> We are often told in negotiations, that the particular plant at the bargaining table is operating at a loss or with minimum profits, even when the consolidated financial statement for the company shows some pretty impressive profit figures.[14]

Senator Hart, Chairman of the Subcommittee hearing this testimony, concluded: "It certainly would appear that conglomerating industry does inevitably beget larger union compositions and structures."[15] This is the same conclusion reached by a former executive of the AFL-CIO: "The best possible situation is one union per industry. . . . But with separate unions, we must come up with methods of dealing with the industrial giants in a coordinate effort."[16] Both of these conclusions follow along the line of Galbraith's concept of countervailing power.

Historically, unions have cooperated in the collective bargaining process. Alliances of union councils, city-wide federations and the like evolved with unionism in the late eighteenth and early nineteenth centuries. As the union movement progressed, national unions were created as combinations of locals. Finally, national and international federations of national unions evolved, the most successful being the AF of L and the CIO which merged in the 1950s to form the AFL-CIO.

There are many fairly recent examples of cooperation between locals of different national unions. One cooperative effort took place in 1956 and involved the major meat packing firms negotiating with a joint committee of the Amalgamated Meat Cutters and Butcher Workmen and the United Packinghouse Workers. In another instance in the late 1950s, the Boot and Shoe Workers Union and the United Shoe Workers of America negotiated jointly with Brown Shoe Company and the International Shoe Company.[17] In the 1960s the Independent Longshoremen and Warehousemen's Union (ILWU) and the Sugar Workers Union held joint negotiation with the California and Hawaiian Sugar Refining Corporation and the ILWU and the Teamsters negotiated jointly with Kaiser Gypsum.[18]

The question that arises at this juncture is why haven't unions joined forces more often in order to tilt the balance of negotiating power in their direction. This begs the broader question of why there are many unions today instead of just a few. The primary explanation, notwithstanding employer opposition and government rules, lies in the heterogeneity of the labor force. There is great diversity in race, sex, education, skills and occupations. In addition, the competitive nature of the various markets of the economy is disparate. Generally speaking, in the more competitive industries, workers are most concerned about job security and justice, whereas, in the less competitive industries, workers tend to be most concerned about their share of the monopoly profits. Even so, there is almost universal agreement among unions that their single most important mission involves the economic well-being of the membership. However, there rarely is a consensus regarding what the most important economic variables are, how negotiations should be handled, what should be compromised, and so on. Unions are not drawn naturally together, therefore, in addition to the obstacles they face in negotiations with firms, they also face obstacles when forming alliances with each other.

A tremendous amount of industrial strife developed when labor attempted to organize in the
nineteenth and early twentieth centuries. One of
the reasons for this, though certainly not the
only one, was that there was no orderly procedure
for determining exactly which employees a union
ought to organize. It became evident that a significant part of the strike activity could be
eliminated by determining exactly who was to be
organized and whether those individuals wanted to
be organized. The problem was resolved with the
passage of the Wagner Act (National Labor Relations Act) in 1935.[19] This Act set up the National
Labor Relations Board (NLRB) which was empowered
to designate the "appropriate" bargaining unit and
then to conduct elections to ascertain whether a
majority of the unit wanted to be unionized. The
Wagner Act left the meaning of "appropriate"
vague. It said that the unit should "insure to
employees the full benefit of their right to self-
organization and collective bargaining."[20] Thus,
from the outset, the NLRB was given the responsibility of determining the appropriateness of the
unit. The NLRB decided that each case was to be
viewed separately under a general set of guidelines. These guidelines included:

1. The history, extent, and type of organization of employees in a plant;
2. The history of their collective bargaining;
3. The history, extent, and type of organization and collective bargaining of employees in other plants of the same employer or
employers in the same industry;
4. The skill, wages, work, and working conditions of employees;
5. The eligibility of employees for membership in the union or unions involved in the
election proceedings and in other labor
organizations;
6. The desires of the employees;
7. The relationship between the unit or
units proposed and the employer's organization, management, and operation of the
firm.[21]

Section 8(a)(5) of the Wagner Act obligated management to bargain with the majority representa-

tive of the bargaining unit.[22] That is, once the
NLRB has designated the appropriate unit, and a
majority of those voting in the certification
election vote for a particular union, management
must bargain with its representatives.

While the definition of the "appropriate" unit
is a rather vague concept and is determined in an
ad hoc manner based on the guidelines listed above,
its definition is much easier to determine than
that of the "appropriate" bargaining structure.
Bargaining structure refers to the types of negotiating units represented on the two sides of the
table. On the labor side, the negotiating unit may
be comprised of one bargaining unit or of several
(joined together to face one firm or a group of
firms). It is the negotiating unit that is crucial
to bargaining power. In order for labor to have a
negotiating unit of equivalent power to that of a
multiproduct firm, the several certified bargaining units of that firm would have to combine and
form one front for negotiating purposes.

Legal problems arise, however, as the NLRB has
designated each unit as the appropriate unit for
collective bargaining (negotiating) purposes. A
combination of these units constitutes a new unit
which, when resisted by firms, makes their legal
existence questionable. A multi-product firm would
like to negotiate with each "appropriate" unit
separately while the unions would rather join
together as one. The NLRB has to determine whether,
given the multi-product nature of a firm, the firm
is obligated to bargain with one negotiating unit
consisting of several bargaining units or whether
it may bargain with each bargaining unit separately. The NLRB, then, is charged with distin-
guishing between units and structure for negotiating purposes, and its decision affects the
balance of power in the bargaining process.

One must also put the scope of bargaining,
which refers to the spectrum of issues that the
parties choose to discuss, into perspective. Before the passage of the Wagner Act, the parties
to a collective negotiation were free to bargain,
not to bargain, or to bargain over some issues
that were mutually agreed upon. With the passage
of the Wagner Act, as amended by the Taft-Hartley
Act in 1947, both sides were charged with the

obligation to "bargain in good faith." The NLRB,
in interpreting this phrase, has generated the
following guidelines:

1. There must be a serious attempt to adjust differences and to reach an acceptable
common ground.
2. Counterproposals must be offered when
one party's proposal is rejected.
3. A position with regard to contract terms
may not be constantly changed.
4. Evasive behavior is not permitted.
5. There must be a willingness to incorporate oral agreements into a written contract.[23]

In 1958, the NLRB had the opportunity to extend
these guidelines by determining the classification
of issues for bargaining purposes. The NLRB, upheld
by the Supreme Court, determined that Section 8(d)
of Taft-Hartley specifies that "to bargain collectively is the performance of the mutual obligation of the employer and the representative of the
employees to . . . confer in good faith with respect to wages, hours, and other terms and conditions of employment."[24] The board's interpretation
of this section was that the scope of bargaining
should be divided into three categories: illegal
items, mandatory items, and voluntary items.[25] If
an item is deemed illegal under the Taft-Hartley
Act, then the side pressing this issue would be
acting illegally under the law. Therefore, the
other side would not be obligated to bargain over
this issue, and the initiating side could not
refuse to sign a contract due to impasse on this
item alone. Mandatory items were those which the
NLRB would include within "wages, hours, and
other items and conditions of employment." The
NLRB, of course, would have to decide whether a
particular issue fell in this category. If an
issue is declared mandatory, then both sides are
obligated to bargain in good faith--to impasse if
necessary--on the issue. In other words, employers
have the right not to sign a contract if such an
issue is not resolved; likewise, unions may strike
over the exclusion or impasse of such issues.
Voluntary items are those issues which are neither
illegal nor mandatory and may not be bargained to
impasse, but brought by unions to the table and
refused by management; the union must accept

management's refusal to bargain. Likewise, if the
union refuses to negotiate such an issue, management cannot refuse to sign the contract solely on
this ground. The NLRB places an issue in either
the illegal or voluntary category, and the side
bringing the issue to the bargaining table must
rely on the other side's amiability in resolving
it. If the other side chooses not to bargain, it
is a dead issue.

Labor has attempted to change the bargaining
structure so that it may gain a position of equal
power when facing conglomerate firms. The result
has been the formation of coalition and/or coordinated bargaining structures. Coalition and coordinated bargaining are similar, but they differ on
a technical point. Coalition bargaining refers "to
the situation where two or more unions bargain
jointly for a common 'master agreement' covering
all the employees which they purport to represent
. . . coordinated bargaining . . . denote(s) the
circumstance where two or more unions representing
separate bargaining units negotiate jointly for
individual unit contracts containing common
terms."[26] The latter refers to separate agreements
while the former refers to a common agreement. This
has become quite significant under the law.

Generally, firms have taken the position that
coalition bargaining is completely illegal. The
Wagner Act, however, does not specifically prohibit an employer from negotiating with a group of
unions representing its employees. Lynn Wagner has
noted "there is a 'minimum of consensus,' at least
that it is lawful for the parties to negotiate on
a coalition basis if they so desire. . . . Analy-
tically, the real issues in the controversy surrounding coalition bargaining are whether a union
can lawfully insist to the point of an impasse in
negotiations that he do so."[27] Thus, under the
Wagner Act, firms are required to bargain with the
majority representative of the appropriate unit
over wages, hours, and other terms and conditions
of employment (mandatory issues). The firms argue
that the unions' demand for coalition bargaining
is a demand for the firm to bargain with an inappropriate bargaining unit (illegal issue) which
it is not obligated to do. Thus Wagner concludes
"there is little reason to believe, therefore,
that the large conglomerate employer will be unsuccessful in his endeavors to escape the compulsions

of Section 8 (a) (5) by maintaining that the coalition represents an inappropriate multi-plant bargaining unit."[28] To date, firms have been successful in resisting coalition bargaining on these grounds.

The central question is whether unions have the right to bargain to impasse on the issue of the bargaining structure. The NLRB has the obligation of determining the "appropriate" unit for collective bargaining purposes and has decided that bargaining over structure is a voluntary issue. Therefore, if management wants a single unit bargaining structure rather than coalition bargaining, unions cannot force the issue to impasse.[29]

The legality surrounding coordinated bargaining is different because there are many separate units bargaining together with the employer but for separate contracts (which may, in fact, be rather similar). Conglomerate firms have also treated this structure as illegal. In this instance the NLRB has held that a firm must bargain with those chosen by the union regardless of whether these include representatives from other units. Further support for this structure was shown when the NLRB, upheld by the Sixth Circuit Court in 1962, ruled that separate units using coordinated bargaining may consider the issue of identical contract termination dates as mandatory.[30] However, one unit may not go to impasse on an issue that just affects another unit in the group.[31] There was a distinction made between having common expiration dates being a mandatory issue when the two want the same, but not mandatory when one unit is going to impasse just to help another. This distinction was eliminated by the courts in 1972.

In 1967-68, there was a strike in the copper industry involving Phelps Dodge. The strike was precipitated by an NLRB ruling that the unions involved had illegally tried to change the structure of the negotiating unit. The decision of the NLRB was appealed to the Courts and, in 1972, the Third Circuit Court reversed the NLRB ruling. In essence, the Court held the following issues to be mandatory, thereby giving the unions the right to bargain to impasse and strike.

1. A demand for common expiration dates for all contracts being negotiated.

2. A posture of simultaneous settlement,
that is, that the unions would not sign
new agreements in any bargaining unit
until negotiations from other bargaining
units had also reached satisfactory set-
tlements.
3. A demand for a limited no-strike clause,
which would permit strikes during the contract at one bargaining unit in support of
employees in another bargaining unit.
4. A demand for a "most favored nations"
clause, providing that existing contracts
may be reopened to incorporate provisions
of any new contracts subsequently agreed
to by the company.[32]

Kenneth Alexander has pointed out that "this
case leaves the impression that unions, striking
for a single set of negotiations or for a single
master contract to cover employees in legally-
separate bargaining units, would evidence an illegal attempt to change the scope of the bargaining
unit."[33] While labor did not accomplish the goal
of legalizing coalition bargaining, it clearly
gained some concessions. Now there are mandatory
issues which involve a coordinated bargaining
structure. This may encourage joint bargaining in
the future and could pave the way for master contract negotiations.

It is interesting that the Court and the NLRB
have disagreed over this issue. Unions, as well as
firms, are operating in an inconsistent environment. The credibility of the NLRB would seem to be
compromised by such reversals. This decision does
imply, though, that coordinated bargaining will be
viewed benignly; thus unions have begun to insti-
tutionalize a new bargaining structure in their
attempt to counter the power of conglomerate
firms.

What led unions to seek a coordinated bargaining structure? "Coordinated bargaining is the
brainchild of the Industrial Union Department
(IUD) of the AFL-CIO."[34] It is the IUD's purpose
to create "centralized, company-wide bargaining
combined with (in a lesser role) local negotiations."[35] After this is accomplished, its goal is
to extend company-wide bargaining to industry-
wide bargaining. The IUD could accomplish this by
using common expiration dates for all contracts

in an industry. Although combination is desirable, it is not actually necessary since the locals having the early expiration dates may choose to work without a contract until the expiration dates of the others are reached. The firms could be faced with legal strikes by all locals. The final outcome could be the formation of new unions which are a combination of several existing unions. These would be "conglomerate" unions, that is, large organizations representing workers of different skills and occupations in different product markets.

Although the IUD is primarily interested in recapturing lost bargaining power, a unique element particular to the scope of bargaining allows for inroads to be made in other areas as well. Firms tend to offer uniform benefits to workers regardless of their union affiliation. Since benefits are company-wide, individual bargaining units have little chance to influence the content of the package offered. As the IUD realized, a coordinated effort involving all bargaining units within a firm would give unions an opportunity to have influence in an area where, heretofore, they had little or none.

The following statement, offered by a representative of the AFL-CIO, summarizes the rationale for the emergence of the IUD.

> It has been out of the necessity to react to these dynamically changing corporation complexes that the labor movement has been led to the development of the coordinated bargaining technique. Through this means we are in the process of developing a structure capable of handling the problems posed by the radically different corporate entities we face.[36]

What evolved after the passage of the Wagner Act in 1935 was a centralization of bargaining power within the union organization. The Act was successful in encouraging the growth of labor unions and this growth led to an increase in economic power within this sector of the economy. Labor leaders, in some instances, responded by wielding this power for the unions' benefit instead of the workers'. (The union has a double

life: it is concerned with its own well-being as
well as the well-being of its workers.)

One of the primary purposes of the Taft-Hartley
Act was to strengthen the position of the individual worker; it sought to give him/her more rights
in the collective bargaining process. Included
were the right to refrain from joining a union,
the right to by-pass the union when filing a grie-
vance, and the right to help determine the importance of the issues brought to the bargaining
table.

As noted, with the emergence of conglomerate
firms, it has become necessary for unions to join
forces and create new bargaining structures.
These "conglomerate" unions, having large consti-
tuencies and focusing on the big picture, throw
the individual worker's status right back to that
of the Wagner era. Guy Farmer, former chairman of
the NLRB, has reservations concerning "conglomerate" union bargaining.[37] He has pointed out that
national labor policy has always been supportive
of unit-by-unit bargaining and that, in the past,
both the Congress and the courts have consistently
supported the idea that unions should always be
free to respond to each unique collective bargaining situation. That is, individual unions
should not be constrained by agreements reached
with other members of a coordinated bargaining
unit when the particular needs of its own members
are in danger of being compromised.

Thus, "conglomerate" unions may now be expected
to withhold decision-making power from the local
level and place it at the centralized (company-
wide/industry-wide) level. William Chernish put it
succinctly:

> When a local union agrees to bind itself to
> the IUD program, it necessarily cedes its
> own authority to reach agreement on any
> issue covered by the program to the steer-
> ing committee or the president's committee.
> . . . The international union faces a simi-
> lar dilemma. In some cases, it is forced to
> abandon goals and policies that it had pre-
> viously held desirable, and is required to
> heed the wishes of the coalition as ex-
> pressed by the president's committee. Thus
> there is a second shift in the decision
> making center in all negotiations: from

local to international, and from international to the coalition's president's committee.[38]

What does the structure of a coordinated bargaining unit look like? Consider the case of General Electric. (A detailed study of G.E. and
coordinated bargaining is included as Appendix B
to this chapter.)

> In March, 1966, 300 delegates from 150 local
> unions, affiliated with eight international
> unions, met in Washington pursuant to a call
> from the international presidents and George
> Meany, president of the AFL-CIO. The purpose
> was to lay plans for joint bargaining with
> G.E. . . .
> At this time, there were more than eighty
> local unions, representing about 150 bar-
> gaining units in G.E. spread throughout the
> nation. . . . These units were spread over
> approximately sixty plants, manufacturing
> scores of different products in thirty
> states. The total union employees consti-
> tuted little more than half of the com-
> pany's work force of 190,000 employees.[39]

It is apparent that the quantity of economic resources allocated through this type of conglomerate bargaining arrangement is quite substantial.
If this arrangement should prevail in the future,
it is conceivable that a tremendous amount of the
economy's resources could be allocated via a
small number of bargaining agreements.

What happens if an impasse is reached in a negotiation with such a bargaining structure? It
clearly would mean that a substantial portion of
the economy's resources could be idled. Chernish
has stated that "coalitionism would tend to increase the likelihood of more frequent, larger
and longer strikes and therefore have an impact
upon the public which cannot be overlooked."[40]

There are provisions of Taft-Hartley that
specifically deal with strikes threatening the
well-being of the economy. Title II of the Act
outlines governmental steps designed to alleviate
any threat to the economy created by a union
strike. The first provision of Title II deals with
offering of federal mediation and conciliation

services to management and labor in the hope that
these services would neutralize the threat of any
"interruptions of the free flow of commerce growing out of labor disputes."[41] If these services
fail to achieve the desired result, Title II makes
provision for the declaration of a national emergency if the health or safety of the economy is
threatened. As the Act states, "Upon receiving a
report from a board of inquiry the President may
direct the Attorney General to petition any district court of the United States having jurisdic-
tion of the parties to enjoin such strike or lock-
out or the continuing thereof (if the court finds
that such will imperil the national health and
safety)."[42] This national emergency provision of
Title II has been used, albeit sparingly. The most
recent occasion was winter, 1977-78, during the
United Mine Workers Strike.

The future may witness an increasingly active
role for government in collective negotiations. If
the bargaining structure tends to become the conglomerate-conglomerate type, then each negotiation
will involve substantial quantities of resources.
Any impasse, real or threatened, could easily come
under these provisions; thus, the probability of
government intervention would be greatly increased.
Over a period of time, government may become a
very active partner in the collective bargaining
process.

There is yet a more subtle way in which centralized control of resources may result from coordinated bargaining. The movement toward this type
of bargaining could take on the appearance of
"enterprise" unionism. Enterprise unions refer to
those which are "oriented toward the employing
unit--the enterprise."[43] This is most common in
Japan where workers generally experience life-long
employment with one firm. The United States analogy
occurs when coordinated bargaining brings together
all the unionized employees of a firm. Hence, the
coordinated efforts of the unions have the result
of orienting the workers toward the employing unit.

Herbert Lahne has noted, "in terms of the structure of unionism in Japan, this link has meant
that to the Japanese worker it is the enterprise
union which is his union. The national unions
there are thus characteristically weak, being
really loose confederations of enterprise unions."[44]
Whether enterprise unionism will evolve remains to

be seen. However, the movement toward conglomerate firms and conglomerate unions leads us in this direction, not away from it.

It is evident that the move by unions to a coordinate type bargaining structure is a response to the conglomerate structure of the firms with which they bargain. Such a change produces more economically powerful unions vis-à-vis managements in the bargaining process. Information to date indicates that coordinated bargaining is considered legal and will probably become more popular in the future.

The variety of results anticipated are that corporate movement to conglomerate status will cause an increase in the concentration of both corporate and union economic power; the union movement to conglomerate status means that the individual worker will probably receive less attention in the future than was intended under recent federal labor legislation; the massive quantities of resources represented by both sides of the table could threaten the well-being of the economy whenever an impasse is reached; and conglomerate-conglomerate bargaining may be responsible for the evolution of enterprise unionism.

Increases in corporate power achieved through diversification have begotten increases in union power through coordination and cooperation. This is the latest in a series of countervailing responses by labor to increases in corporate bargaining power. While earlier responses by labor unions may have caused the emergence of the powerful national unions, this current response may cause the emergence of powerful enterprise unions.

5 The Evolution of Capitalism

EVOLUTIONARY principles are usually associated
with Charles Darwin and the biological sciences.
The basic premise of evolutionary theory is that
systems are constantly undergoing change and that
this change does not have any prior intention of
going in any particular direction or to any particular end. Evolutionary economists have used
this theory in studying economic systems and believe that our economic system is constantly
changing, but toward no particular long-run position. The use of evolutionary economic theory
allows us to evaluate the nature of a system and
predict in which direction that system seems to
be moving. Obviously it is not an exact science,
but its use can narrow a broad spectrum of possibilities to a manageable few. Applying evolutionary economic theories to the emergence of conglomerate firms, one can identify those few evolutionary paths that have the highest likelihood
of being the future path our system will take.

In order to discuss an evolutionary approach, a
brief background analysis is necessary. Mainstream
economics today derives its theoretical base from
the fundamental tenets of the physical sciences of
physics and chemistry. It is within these sciences
that such concepts as equilibrium, natural laws,
stability, and motion exist. Stable equilibrium
and comparative statics are stressed. The mainstream economist tries to establish logical,
mathematical models as a physicist or chemist
would. The only difference is that chemists or
physicists can control the environment in which
they do research and, therefore, can invoke

ceteris paribus as a legitimate process in experi-
mentation. Economists, on the other hand, deal
with the economy as their laboratory and thus,
pragmatically speaking, cannot hold certain variables constant while changing others.

The tenets of physics and chemistry as a foundation for mainstream economic theory has not gone
unchallenged. A dissenting movement in the profes-
sion embraces the tenets of the biological sciences as the appropriate foundation for economic
theory. These dissenters subscribe to a philosophy
known as institutionalism.[1] Institutionalist evolutionary thought derives from the philosophy that
static, equilibrium, test-tube analysis is illegit-
imate for studying economic activity. The logic is
that the economy is dynamic in nature; any theory
used to describe it must deal with dynamics, not
statics. The economy is not subject to the qualification ceteris paribus; an economist cannot observe
changes under laboratory conditions; the variables
in our models do not remain equal and unchanging,
but they undergo constant change.

The concept of evolution originated in the biological sciences with the advent of Charles Darwin's On the Origin of Species. Darwin argued that
evolution was the force from which the universe
operates. Evolution has two basic premises: the
world is in a constant process of change, and this
continuum of change does not have any apparent
prior intention of going along a specific path or
evolving to a particular end. The institutionalists
subscribe to this theory because they believe the
economy is subject to cumulative change--what
Gunnar Myrdal has called "circular causation."[2]
Circular causation means that once a change has
taken place in the economic system, it will cause
other conditions to change. These secondary changes,
in turn, will cause even further changes, not the
least of which will be to affect the change that
initiated this sequence. In short, the whole system is constantly in motion.

With regard to conglomerates and market structure, an institutionalist might suggest that
forces must have been present in the economy to
cause firms to seek diversification, and that
these forces allowed for the eventual evolution of
conglomerates. As this occurred, the institutionalist would argue that it became a force which
would eventually cause the economy to undergo

other changes. The key is that the emergence of
conglomerates should give institutionalists the
ability to recognize the change in economic structure that has evolved and to perceive in what
direction this event will take the system in the
future.

The ever changing nature of our dominant firms
prompts one to search for understanding through
the techniques of evolution rather than those of
equilibrium. In studying the evolution of the
economic system, one must focus on the economy as
a whole. "To focus on the economy is to ask how
the economy makes choices, what emergent values
economic choices reflect, how the choices are con-
ditioned and shaped, in what direction the economy
appears to be headed, and with what consequences."[3]
For this purpose, one must evaluate the emergence
of conglomerates according to how it reflects the
needs of the corporate enterprise. Further analysis is needed to ascertain what changes in decision-making take place as conglomerates take over
a dominant role in the economy. Finally, the question that must be addressed is what will conglomerate movement lead to--in terms of economic struc-
ture--in the long-run, and how will this new structure respond to the needs of the collective society.

The evolutionary approach requires that a rea-
listic set of parameters be used when evaluating
capitalism. Since the current market structure is
not one of many small firms, but one of a few
large conglomerates, it is incorrect to evaluate
the current structure using eighteenth-century
notions of competition. The evaluation of the performance of the economy should be based on the
actual nature of the system, not the theoretical.

The evolutionary process of capitalism has produced a concentration of power in our system.
Several very large firms and labor unions have
emerged. Concentrated power allows for entities in
the economy to affect change as well as being
affected by it. Since power exists, one is required
to incorporate this variable within the analytical
framework which describes the economy. Power also
affects change in the political arena and vice
versa. The results that might evolve from concentrated power have to be analyzed so that any
change brought about within the society due to
this power can be identified and evaluated.

Finally, an evolutionary approach must scrutinize the goals of society so that an evaluation can be made. Both the economy and society's goals are ever changing, thus, the trick is to identify current goals and match them to the current performance of the economy. To use antiquated goals and match them with contemporary performance is incorrect. The goals of contemporary society must be coupled with the current structure and performance of the economy, for only then can there be any chance of ascertaining whether the outcomes of our system are those which are desired.

As the American colonies moved toward independence in the late eighteenth century, the economy was characterized predominately by individual proprietorships. The philosophy that dominated the early republic was that of the earlier French Revolution. Liberty was the cornerstone; the vehicle that propelled it was private property. Thomas Jefferson's view of the economy epitomized this philosophy. His ideal was one in which private property was universal, no one was very rich or very poor.[4] Thus, in the beginning economic activity was based on a structure of atomistic firms relying on the forces of the market for their direction and success.

This structure was compatible with the prevailing economic theories of the day. Adam Smith's Wealth of Nations was easily the most influential theory. In markets, Smith argued, competition would prevail. Entrepreneurs would compete and, thus, control one another through their interactions. The competitive element would check inequalities, force efficiency in production, and prevent the accumulation of economic power. It is interesting to note that Smith considered the corporate entity and found it wholly unsuited for survival in a market economy. He argued that no one would ever pay as much attention to other men's affairs as he would to his own. Therefore, in a competitive situation, corporations would not be as prepared to compete as would individual proprietorships. Except for certain government sponsored activities, corporations would not survive.[5] Obviously, Smith did not forsee a management staff evolving that could maximize its own well-being through corporate employment.

Although Smith championed the competitive market system, he did so recognizing that limitations

on restraining the self-interest of the entrepreneur existed. "People of the same trade seldom
meet together, even for merriment and diversion,
but the conversation ends in conspiracy against
the public or in some contrivance to raise price."[6]
This often quoted sentiment indicates his distrust
of the prime motivators of this economic system.
Our forefathers shared this distrust, for they
attempted to deny the possibility of an economic
structure evolving that would facilitate conspiracy.

The convention that met to draw up the United
States Constitution in 1787 considered the question of whether the federal government should be
allowed the power to bestow corporate status upon
firms. It was decided that corporations would have
more power relative to individual proprietorships
and that this may be harmful to competition.[7] In
addition, the convention's participants recognized
that corporate entities could easily become monopolies. Corporate legality was disallowed largely on
account of its potential for devastating the economy.

The framers of the Constitution did not take
into consideration the possibility of individual
states allowing for corporate charters. They
assumed the states would follow the federal lead;
they were wrong. By 1800, there were 355 profit-
making, state-chartered corporations. The majority
of these, 255 were public purpose corporations
(utilities) and 67 were financial in nature. Only
six were manufacturing concerns.[8] However, both
state and federal laws were passed to limit the
scope and power of these corporate entities. The
laws generally provided that corporations could
hold only a limited amount of land, could produce
single products only, and could exist for a speci-
fied period of time. The reasons for these restric-
tions were obvious. Legislators clearly wanted to
assure that corporations would not grow so large
that they would be more powerful than the single
proprietorships with which they competed. Prohibiting geographic expansion was obviously necessary. Also, not allowing corporations to exist for
long periods of time meant that they could not
accumulate vast sums of money through retained
earnings. To allow these things to occur would
permit the eradication of the Jeffersonian economic
structure.

The technological breakthroughs that were responsible for the coming of the railroads were also responsible for solidifying the corporate institution in the economic system. The first major railroad corporation, the New York Central Railroad, was formed in the early 1850s.[9] The huge capital costs incurred in building the railroads were sufficient to demonstrate the need for corporations. Competition between railroads was so severe in the latter part of the nineteenth century that it gave way to cooperation. At first, railroad corporations formed trusts. Later these were outlawed and, finally, the corporations merged and were regulated by government. By 1930, fourteen railroad companies accounted for 82% of all track mileage in the country.[10]

Because railroads had been successful at incorporation, other firms began to follow suit. The last half of the nineteenth century, particularly after the Civil War, witnessed a rapid increase in the number of corporations. The subtlety was that ownership and control of assets were slowly being transferred in the economy. With corporations, the dichotomy of the passive and the active participants in the economic arena was introduced. In Jeffersonian capitalism, all participants had been active. The owners of the means of production managed their assets and competed with other owner-managers. With the advent of the corporation, the owners (stockholders) became passive, and the corporation acquired managers who were not owners. This is one of the major institutional changes brought about by the legalization of the corporate entity. By the end of the nineteenth century, corporations had achieved all the rights the forefathers of the constitution had desired to deny them. They could own property unrelated to production, they could produce many products, and their longevity was assured.

Corporations were legitimate, but this was just the beginning. The latter part of the nineteenth century ushered in the great trusts. Horizontal mergers took place between competitors in all the major manufacturing industries. Pools and trusts were the common denominator of the day. The public was quite intimidated by these large, powerful trusts and consequently demanded their dissolution. The Sherman Act was passed in 1890 to prohibit monopolies and restraint of trade. The economic

structure, however, was not much changed by the
antitrust legislation. Large corporations persisted; the "good and reasonable trusts," and the
economy of the Jeffersonian era was lost, apparently forever.[11]

The crash of the stock market and the ensuing
Securities and Exchange Act of 1934 brought a halt
to the growth of the trusts.[12] Even though the
trusts were outlawed, the structure of the economy
had been permanently changed. Between the 1930s
and the end of the 1950s the overall structure of
the manufacturing sector of the economy generally
remained unchanged; the rapid increase in aggregate concentration that persisted between 1860 and
1930 was lessened.[13]

What has evolved in place of dominant firms in
particular industries is the dominance of firms
over the entire economy. The manufacturing sector
has been dominated by a few large firms since the
turn of the century. Moreover, a significant change
has taken place in the composition of those firms.
Presently these firms are continuously diversifying. Their multi-product nature weakens the meaning of market concentration ratios based on 4-firm,
4-digit industry definitions. Diversified firms
can dominate a network of economic activity whether
they dominant particular markets or not. Indeed,
conglomerate firms may not have any desire to
dominate particular markets. Because of the antitrust laws, they may avoid dominating markets. However, their desire for growth is no different than
that of the early corporations--the trusts. It is
only the nature of the growth that is different.

What evolutionary path does the emergence of
conglomerates portend for the economy? The introduction of a network of firms that compete with
each other over a span of markets critically alters
the structure of the economy. Theories generated
by evolutionary economists can be used to predict
the path that capitalism will take. These theories
postulate that firm growth and organizational
change are a function of accumulation, innovation,
financial management, political incentives, and
technological breakthroughs. While each theory
emphasizes one of these as the driving force behind growth and organizational change, all are
tied by the common presumption that firms seek
growth and change as a vehicle for power. The
natural tendency of an enterprise competing in a

capitalistic system is to grow since growth is rewarded by market, economic, conglomerate, and
political power.

As already noted, the economic structure which
spawned conglomerates was hardly atomistic. It was
basically a structure of large firms dominating
particular markets. One theory that could add insight to the evolution of conglomerates would be
based on the premise that it facilitates a further centralization of the means of production.
This Marxian approach to economic activity is of a
quasi-evolutionary nature. It is evolutionary in
the sense that the Marxists see economic activity
starting with slavery and evolving through several
stages, capitalism being one, and with the final
stage being communism.[14] What makes this quasi-
evolutionary is that while the Marxists envision a
series of changes, they also see a beginning and
an end. There is an ultimate economic organization
in their scheme of things. Evolutionary thought
does not have such a thesis. It is open-ended; the
economy will be continuously going through changes
with no "final" stage expected.

Given that Marxian theory is quasi-evolutionary,
it does provide insights into the workings of capitalism. The Marxian approach holds that firms are
driven to accumulate capital in order to maintain
their competitive position in the marketplace.
Ironically, this accumulation of capital forces a
falling rate of profit and the elimination of marginal firms while the surviving firms increase
their size through continued accumulation. This
causes a centralization of the means of production
as a few large corporations eventually dominate
the economy. Up to this point Marxian thought
would not be incompatible with how the economic
structure of our economy has evolved over the
last 200 years.

However, the centralization of the means of
production is but one part of the overall Marxian
scheme. Marxists would also argue that the dominance of the economy by a few, large firms would
lead to conflict between the capitalist and labor
classes. Thus, class struggle becomes an intricate
part of the evolutionary process. Conflict is derived from the interaction of the forces and the
relations of production. The forces of production
constitute society's technology, that is, labor
skills, knowledge, tools, and capital.[15] The rela-

tions of production comprise the economic structure of society. They are the rules of the game
which give rise to the legal and political arrangements in society. The relations of production in a
capitalistic system are predicated on the existence of private property, so conflict arises due
to the nature of these forces and relations of
production. The forces of production are dynamic
in nature while the relations of production are
static. Thus, the ever changing nature of the
forces of production will eventually cause an in-
compatibility with private property (the epitome
of the relations of production). As long as capitalism exists, the rights of private property will
dominate. Eventually, the dynamic forces will
cause such a centralization of the means of production that a class struggle will ensue between
the few owners of capital and the many, disen-
franchised, alienated laborers. Finally, the working class will seek to change the relations or
production; they will press to eliminate private
property. Ultimately, capitalism will pass and
socialism will evolve.

There is some disagreement among Marxists regarding the actual nature of the evolution. Some
argue that it will be violent, others do not. Each
side of this debate offers supporting evidence.
The revolutions in Russia and China were violent,
the move toward socialism in Great Britain was
peaceful. Regardless of the nature of the change,
both sides agree that capitalism will not last and
will eventually give way due to the conflict between technology and society.

Marxist theory provides that economic power is
primary in a capitalist economy and that political
power is both its offspring and its servant.[16]
A logical extension is that the political arena is
dominated by the interests of the capitalist class
and that labor interests are thus subservient.
With a heightening of labor unrest, the revolution
that should take place will occur via an overthrow
of the capitalists' political and economic systems.
Within our present systems, such a confrontation
between labor and capital does not seem imminent.
In fact, the very nature of our political and
economic systems would seem to preclude such an
outcome. There are two basic factors at work here.
First, the laboring class is heterogeneous. Half
is white collar, hence skilled, and many of the

blue collar are skilled as well. These workers
have not identified with the Marxian class-strug-
gle. Second, the two predominant political parties
in the United States are comprised of many interest groups, corporations and labor being but two.
Neither of the parties could afford to allow itself to be dominated by any one interest group.
Therefore, the lack of class identification coupled with the structural arrangement of our political parties reduces the probability of a class
conflict struggle that leads to revolution.

It is quite obvious, though, that there are a
few large diversified firms that dominate the manufacturing sector of the economy. Since the class
conflict argument does not seem to be applicable,
the question arises as to whether the evolution of
capitalism to socialism is inevitable if it is
based solely on a centralization of the means of
production. This will depend on whether the dynamic nature of capitalism that has produced conglomerates is compatible with the current relations of production. If conglomerate firms tend
to yield a stable, near fully employed economy
over a period of time, then the status quo of the
legal and social systems may be preserved. On the
other hand, if these results are not forthcoming,
then the Marxian revolutionary consequences may be
the outcome.

Another quasi-evolutionary approach that may
lend insight into the nature of the evolution of
capitalism has to do with innovation and innovators. This approach is also classified as quasi-
evolutionary since it is derived from Schumpeterian
postulates; Joseph Schumpeter believed that capitalism was headed toward a precise outcome: socialism.[17] Similar to the Marxists, he foresaw continuous change during capitalism's reign, but that
socialism was inevitable as the final outcome of
the economic process.

This approach ties together innovators with
business cycles and argues that these two elements
are inherently part of a capitalist structure.
Cycles begin their upswing when something "new" is
introduced into the economy. The innovation could
be a technological breakthrough, a new product, a
new source of supply, or a new type of organizational structure.[18] Regardless of its form, it
would initiate increased economic activity. This
would eventually lead to what Schumpeter called

"creative destruction."[19] Firms would have a
choice, given the introduction of the "new" element, of either adopting it into their own production processes or of being competitively destroyed.
Thus, the innovation has both creative and destruc-
tive aspects. Destruction is good because it eliminates marginal, unprofitable firms. Economic
recessions result as the digestion of the innovation works its way through the economy. When
another innovation takes place, the cycle repeats
itself.

Conglomerates may be considered a new form of
business organization and could be the key element
necessary to generate a new round of growth in the
economy. Moreover, the theory of creative destruction could explain why more firms are seeking to
diversify. They must either adapt to the new conglomerate structure or they will not survive. Some
observers have viewed this as defensive behavior
while others have considered it to be faddish. In
either case, it fits in this framework.

A Schumpeterian approach, then, holds that
innovations within the capitalistic system bring
economic gains to that system. It follows that if
any force within the system created an environment
that negated innovation, then the dynamic nature
of capitalism would be threatened. The very
nature of a conglomerate structure is such that it
may strengthen capitalism in the short run but
threaten its very existence in the long run. There
has to exist a unique environment in order for
innovations to persist. Innovation is a function
of the number of innovators in the system; the number of innovators is a function of the relationship of reward to risk in the economic system. If
an individual innovator feels that the environment
will yield a sufficient reward commensurate with
the risk involved in undertaking the project, then
the innovation will occur. However, if the arrangement of the economy is such that this is not true,
then innovations and innovators will cease to
exist. The supply of innovators, then, becomes the
key element.

The case can be made that there is currently a
supply of innovators in the conglomerate area.
Entrepreneurs that put together such firms as Gulf
and Western, Ling-Temco-Vought and ITT have been
described as innovators and risk takers. The decision by such entrepreneurs to diversify on a large

scale could lead to a new round of economic activity. But, the nature of this innovation may cause a different outcome in the future. As this new innovation works its way through the economy, it is digested and the system awaits a new innovation. The organization of these firms, however, has undergone a change. By its very nature the conglomerate firm has a bureaucratic management structure; each addition of a subsidiary to the conglomerate adds more middle and upper level managers. It becomes increasingly difficult in this new environment for innovators to exist because management teams replace individual managers. In addition, larger entities evolving require larger sums of capital to affect change. Larger amounts of capital mean riskier investments, therefore, the cost of introducing a nonprofitable innovation is higher. If this is the path that the conglomerate firm is causing the economy to take, and if the theory of innovators and innovation is correct, then the upturn in activity generated through diversification could be one of the last gasps of capitalism before it drives out innovators and turns to a "managed" economy of bureaucrats.

Considering this approach in terms of the evolution of capitalism, one can hypothesize as to where conglomerate firms might lead the economy. Conglomerate organization of corporations is an innovation that could lead to an upturn in economic activity. It may be the catalyst for another round of economic activity in a continuing chain of innovations within the capitalistic structure. However, while it can be classified as an innovation, it may also be the catalyst which changes the structure of capitalism such that innovations become fewer and fewer. This could threaten the existence of our capitalistic system.

One of the cornerstones of evolutionary thought is the premise that capitalism has within it an inherent dichotomy of value. This idea was suggested by Thorstein Veblen. Studying the capitalistic system, he observed that two sets of values were present. First was the obvious value placed on physical production: maximization of output and efficiency in production were the responsibilities of the engineers and technicians. Second was the value placed on the goods as measured by monetary units: the price associated with a good. Veblen believed that this dichotomy of values was

wrenching the system. He argued that the two values were incompatible, hence, one would have to
dominate the other. His conclusion was that the
monetary measure of value dominated the physical.
The dominant force in the economy was profits;
making money, not output, was paramount. The success of a firm was measured by how much higher
price was relative to cost.[20]

It was Veblen's view, given the dominance of
the profit motive in this system, that the value
system spawned the emergence and growth of large
production units. Corporations evolved because
they were organizational entities that could best
maximize profits. For a firm to be successful
over the long run, obviously, it must be profitable, so corporations facilitated this by regarding efficiency as a secondary value. In fact,
there was a "conscientious withdrawal of efficiency" in the production process when firms
wanted to raise prices.[21] This is the classic
example of a monopolist adjusting output to demand
such that the difference between price and cost is
greatest and profits are maximized. The business-
man's interest in profits dominated the technicians' and engineers' interest in efficiency.

Veblen also recognized the rise of the modern
corporation state and described this as the evolution of "absentee ownership."[22] The stockholders
owned the corporation but were absent from the
workings of the firm. Although managers were not
owners, they now made essential decisions and permitted money values to dominate production values.
Another institutional change involved the rise of
sophisticated finance and credit. Financial transactions of large magnitude evolved as large banks
become more prevalent in the economy. This further
emphasized the "money making" philosophy over the
"production making" philosophy.

The emergence of conglomerates may be explained
as a new kind of organizational structure that
secures the long-run profitability of the firm.
Conglomerates are quite similar to the trusts that
Veblen wrote about at the turn of the century.
The financial nature of the conglomerate is quite
similar to that of the trusts. Financial incentives, manipulation of P/E ratios, synergy, and/or
financial raiding, can induce the emergence of a
conglomerate. Indeed, today's businessmen who are
responsible for the conglomerate movement may

readily be identified with the captains of industry of yesteryear.

Finally, there is the Veblenian premise that
the laissez faire, private-property capitalism of
his day could not sustain itself indefinitely.
Eventually those who valued real production over
monetary production, notably the engineers and
technicians, would push for reforms and for a
dominant position in the decision-making processes
of the large corporations. Though Veblen's hope
was that those technicians and engineers would be
successful reformers, he was not at all confident
that they would succeed. He discerned in society's
value a tendency toward subservience to and emula-
tion of the affluent owners of the corporations.
This encouraged the continued control by the entre-
preneurial class over the economic system.[23] One
possible scenario that might emerge involves the
capitalists allying with the political organizations of the day in order to remove any threat
posed by the technicians and the engineers.[24]
However, the cost is high since the capitalists
could possibly be giving away their control to
the state.

How does this theory tie in with the conglomerate movement that is currently underway? The
strongest link emerges from the financial theory.
The managers of conglomerates have made extensive
use of financial techniques in their pursuit of
increased earnings, and these techniques have permitted financial growth even when no physical
growth was experienced. The variety in accounting
methods which are legal today and the diverse
philosophies that abound make such financial
wizardry attractive. The pyramiding, pooling, and
stock manipulations of the era of the great trusts
are being duplicated, in quality, if not in quantity, by synergy, P/E leverage, hidden asset acquisition, and pension fund raiding. Galbraith's re-
ferral to the great trusts of the 1920s as extra-
vagant arrangements maximizing financial leverage
at every turn could also be representative of
conglomerates today. Conglomerates continue to use
those same financial techniques to facilitate
earnings growth and stock price appreciation, and
they may be considered organizations that appre-
ciate the ledger more than the machine.

One function of government is to establish the
legal framework within which an economic system

operates. Once this framework is in place, governance administers to the needs of the consuming
and producing public. All economic actors--firms,
laborers, and consumers--are interested in governance since it has the role of sanctioning or prohibiting economic behavior; therefore, they seek
political power: the ability to influence and per-
suade the governing body to pass laws that favor
their interests. Some institutionalists have
argued that economic power begets political
power.[25] This is slightly different from the
Marxian theory which holds that economic power
and political power are synonomous.

In connection with the efforts of economic
actors to obtain political power, John R. Commons
argued that capitalism was predicated upon the
institutional arrangements of corporations, labor
unions, and political interest groups. Transactions between these groups provided the basis of
all economic activity. Commons separated these
transactions into three categories: bargaining,
rationing, and managerial.[26] A bargaining transac-
tion refers to a negotiation between parties having equal status (power). In this type of transac-
tion no coercion is found. Rationing transactions
occur when ownership is transferred based on
authority rather than exchange. Examples of these
transactions are found when unions set wages for
individual workers and when corporations allocate
budgets to their numerous divisions. Finally, managerial transactions, which are also authorita-
tive, refer to exchanges between management and
workers. Commons argued that the evolution of
capitalism involved a continually increasing number of rationing and managerial transactions and
a declining number of bargaining transactions. His
reasoning was based on his observation that capitalism evolved from a Jeffersonian system to one
of large corporations, unions, and government.
With the demise of Jeffersonian capitalism came
the demise of bargaining; with the emergence of
predominately large corporations, unions, and
government, more rationing and managerial transactions occurred.

Commons argued that with the emergence of powerful groups, an individual's rights would be pro-
tected only if he joined one of these groups. In
this way, collective action yields collective free-
dom. Actually, several political scientists have

held that interest groups have evolved (for the
good of the society) because "a single voice may
not be heard except through the binding together
of like-minded persons."[27] This leads one to expect the evolution of capitalism to produce large
economic units which would vie for the limited resources of the economy. The key lies in obtaining
as much legal leverage as possible. Thus, corporations and unions become interest groups and spend
a great deal of money trying to influence the
legal framework within which they operate. Their
goal is to have the balance of power tilted in
their direction so that bargaining transactions
can give way to their own rationing and/or managerial transactions. To this end, firms and unions
spend vast sums of money on political campaigns
and lobbying. Regarding political campaign expenditures, corporations and unions are using political action committees (PACs) to solicit contributions and expend monies in political campaigns.[28]
As Herbert Alexander notes, PACs are viable entities for corporations and unions to use because
they (corporations and unions) include large
groups of like-minded persons, and they have
ready-made channels for communicating with their
numbers.[29]

The regulations regarding PACs have been in
flux for some time. In 1972 the PACs were governed
by the 1971 Federal Election Campaign Act which
stated that corporations and labor organizations
were allowed to fund the cost of PACs but were not
to make contributions to them.[30] Looking at the
Appendix Tables C and D, one can see evidence of
the efforts made by corporations and unions to
influence the election process during the 1972
election campaign. Appendix Table C shows the fund-
ing efforts of the major corporate PACs during
this campaign. As is obvious from the table, the
overwhelming amount of funds raised went to the
Republican candidate, Richard Nixon. This is not
surprising since businessmen felt their needs
would be given more consideration by President
Nixon than by Senator McGovern. Appendix Table D,
which contains the union PACs, has the opposite
outcome. The unions supported the Democratic tick-
et in overwhelming proportions. These two groups
have determined which candidate would be more
likely to tilt the rules in their direction and
allocated their funds accordingly.

By the time of the 1976 federal elections, the regulations regarding PACs had changed. Alexander noted that the 1974 campaign finance change which limited the amount an individual could contribute to a candidate to $1,000 would reduce the role of the large individual contributor and, at the same time, increase the role of the corporation, labor union, and other special interest groups.[31]

In 1975, the Sun Oil Company desired to set up a PAC (SUN PAC) and requested guidance from the Federal Election Commission (FEC). The FEC was established in 1974 as part of an amendment to the 1972 Federal Election Campaign Act.[32] The FEC allowed that Sun Oil could set up and administer SUN PAC out of their general treasury funds as long as the funds were segregated from the firm.[33] In addition, the FEC indicated that SUN PAC could solicit contributions from stockholders and employees but could not solicit the general public (SUN PAC could accept monies from the general public).[34]

In 1976 the Supreme Court ruled in Buckley vs. Valeo that "corporate and union resources may be employed to administer PAC funds and to solicit contributions from employees, stockholders and union members."[35] The Supreme Court also upheld the guidelines in 18 U.S.C.(608(b)(2)) regarding maximum contributions by a PAC.[36] Under the law, a PAC cannot contribute more than $5000 to any one federal candidate.[37] However, the court also held that any corporation or union is within its rights to set up as many PACs as it wishes. Thus, a proliferation of PACs could take place, and the result eliminates the effectiveness of the $5000 maximum.

Finally, and most importantly, the Court also held that once a PAC has contributed to five or more federal candidates, it "can make unlimited independent expenditures . . . on behalf of a candidate."[38] "Independent" refers to expenditures that are not authorized or requested by the candidate, or by the candidate's committee or agent.

The importance of the Sun Oil and Buckley vs. Valeo decisions are obvious: one, PACs can be financed by firms and unions; two, PACs can solicit employees, stockholders, and union workers; three, more than one PAC can be organized by a firm or union; and four, PACs, once they have contributed to five federal candidates, are limited

only by their own budget constraints in expending
funds in support of a candidate.

Such structural changes as firm diversification and union coordination could facilitate a
proliferation of PACs. Firms could have each of
their subsidiaries form PACs, and union-coordinated
groups could form PACs that are independent of
those created by their respective national organizations. Herbert Alexander observed that

> a dramatic increase in political contribu-
> tions by special interest groups . . . could
> be clearly charted both in the 1974 off-year
> congressional elections and the 1976 elec-
> tion campaign. . . . Some 242 new committees--
> 30 percent of all interest group committees
> registered under the federal law--had been
> formed for the presidential campaign year
> 1976. About three out of four of these new
> committees had been formed by business re-
> lated interests.[39]

About 15% of the new committees were labor related.[40] Appendix Table E shows the leading corporate PACs in the 1976 election. The top three
are affiliated with three of the firms noted in
chapter 3 as being quite diversified.

Concerning congressional contributions in 1976,
Appendix Table F shows that business and labor
were the major contributors, having almost equal
expenditures. Russell Pittman has hypothesized
that highly concentrated industries which were
either subject to federal regulation (utilities,
transportation, media, and industries subject to
EPA), government purchases or to antitrust inves-
tigation would increase the amount of their campaign contributions in times of a national election.[41] Using data for the 1972 presidential election, he found that "among concentrated industries,
national regulation, government purchases and
antitrust investigations are all associated with
increases in industry contributions."[42] Pittman
concluded that, where the government's role is
substantial in an industry, the individuals representing the firms in that industry will "attempt
to win political influence through political contributions."[43]

There is some disagreement regarding the effec-
tiveness of spending money on election campaigns.

Edwin Epstein argues that, regardless of the sum
spent, neither labor nor large corporations have
had an impressive record in getting their candidates elected.[44] This view is rebutted by the work
of Kristian Palda who found a direct and significant correlation between campaign expenditures and
winning elections. Palda concluded that "campaign
expenditures are as important to political candidates as advertising expenditures are to a firm
promoting a product."[45] Even if campaign expenditures are as important as Palda suggests, there
is still the question of whether, once elected,
the politician can or will deliver for the firm or
labor organization. Since they are but two interests in a socially pluralistic system, it is never
assured that their particular concerns will be
vital to the politicians they support.

A more viable alternative for the achievement
of political power is lobbying. It is in their
day-to-day meetings that politicians govern. While
election support suggests infrequent influence in
the political process, the interest group that
lobbies is participating in governance every day.
In addition, during the election campaign, the
interest group must compete with other interest
groups in achieving their electoral goals. This
is not so with lobbying since only a subset will
have an interest in a particular issue. Finally,
election campaign contributions are limited by
law and closely scrutinized by government. Lobbying is the more frequent, more focused, and more
liberated vehicle. Indeed, Alexander has hypothesized that "if campaign contributions are limited
by law, they (representations of commerce, industry, trade association, labor unions, and other
groups) may turn to more sophisticated lobbying."[46]

Lester Salamon and John Siegfried have postulated that a positive relationship exists between
economic size and political activity since the
smaller the firm, the less political expenditures
it can bear and thus the fewer the benefits it can
expect.[47] Similarly, the larger the enterprise,
the more it can afford to spend and the more benefits it can expect to receive. In studying this
proposition empirically, Salamon and Siegfried
found a positive, statistically significant relationship between firm size and degree of lobbying.[48] This result is supported by the work of the
National Industrial Conference Board (NICB) which

found that 32% of the large companies (more than
5,000 employees) had lobbying offices in Washington,
D.C., while 7.5% of medium size companies (1,000-
4,999 employees) and 2% of small firms (500 to 999
employees) had such offices.[49] The NICB also found
that 53% of the large corporations paid "continuous" attention to federal legislation as opposed
to 35% for medium and small firms.[50] Raymond Bauer,
Ithiel de Sola Poole, and Lewis Dexter found that
men from large firms were always more active in
lobbying activities than men from smaller firms.[51]
In fact, they found "in most instances, the most
interested men from the smallest firms were less
active than the least interested men from the
largest firms."[52] In addition, executives of
larger firms tended to have their own positions
staffed so that they would be better informed on
current events and have as part of their mission
to be active in affairs external to the firm.[53]

Salamon and Siegfried also addressed the relationship of geographic disperson to political
power. They found that the more geographically
dispersed were the members of an industry, the
more influence the industry had on Congress.[54]
This result, although not statistically significant, is important to any discussion of conglomerate firms. It could be argued that the more diversified a firm, the more dispersed will be its
geographic locations of production and thereby
the greater its political power. In fact, the
Roundtable, a lobbying organization comprised of
the largest firms in the United States, has acknowledged that one of their very successful lobbying
strategies has involved using corporate executives
from a Congressman's home district to lobby that
Congressman.[55] Since conglomerate firms span many
congressional districts, such a strategy could
enhance their political power.

The capitalistic system is replete with conflict between the various actors in the economy.
Those actors that are best suited for the battle
over the economy's resources will get the most
from it. In the evolutionary process, corporations
become more powerful than single proprietorships.
Unions evolve to counter corporate power. Conglomerates evolve as a new organization that can
better deal with its competing organizations, and
enterprise unions emerge to better deal with conglomerates. It follows that conglomerate firms and

conglomerate unions may be considered manifesta-
tions of a socially pluralistic system. As Cicero
observed, no place is so strongly fortified that
money cannot capture it.

It has been argued that society is characterized as having two forces--the institutional and
the technological.[56] The institutional forces
within society are those static elements that reinforce the status quo, that is, they preserve the
inherent distribution of income, class structure,
and cultural values of society. Technological
forces are the dynamic elements within society
resulting from scientific knowledge which is ever
expanding our frontiers. The increased level of
the state of the arts and its implementation into
the productive process causes conflict between
technology and institutions. The continuous change
demanded by innovation threatens the status quo,
and the institutional forces resist these changes
at every turn. Clarence Ayres believed that the
process of assimilating new technology into the
institutional framework should be the primary
focus of economic analysis. The nature of the
adaptation of the institutional forces to technological change would determine the evolutionary
process of the system. The two forces exist in all
types of systems and their interaction determines
the path of change.

The stronger the forces of institutions, the
slower the rate of change. Conversely, the stronger
the forces of technology, the faster the rate of
change. What is the nature of these technological
forces? Ayres argued that technology is characterized by "know-how, skills and tools."[57] Technology,
then, refers to scientific research, development,
and innovation. If one believes in an evolutionary
path of capitalism, it would follow that the technology introduced by the industrial revolution
would explain the change from Jeffersonian to
monopoly capitalism. Large scale enterprises were
more technologically desirable and necessary for
the successful implementation of the new technology. However, the large size of the enterprises
dictated more funds for operation and greater
risks due to the quantities of resources involved.
Thus, the technology of the industrial revolution
created the need for what Ayres and other institutionalists have called "financial capitalism."
Following Veblen, Ayres argued that monetary value

diverged from industrial production value and that
the dominance of "financial capitalism" made the
importance of science and innovation for progress
secondary to profits, savings, and investment.[58]

Ayres believed that the dominance of "financial
capitalism" could not prohibit technological
change from occurring. Further, as technological
change continued, the financial capitalists would
be threatened with eventual extinction. Here the
financial capitalists comprise an institution in
the economy and therefore wish to assure the status quo, thus setting up the confrontation between
finance and technology. The relative degree of
power held by each side determines when and by
what amount "financial capitalism" undergoes evolutionary change. There is no question of whether
the change will take place; it is inevitable. The
dynamic nature of technology will require change
regardless of the institutional forces opposing it.

Ayres also supported the proposition that
"financial capitalism" is inherently an unstable
arrangement. He said that the "ever-accelerating
pace" of technological change brings "ever-increas-
ing strain" to the economy.[59] This causes instability which manifests itself as economic depression. To alleviate this element of instability
within the system, planning could be introduced.
According to Ayres, "planning is itself a manifestation of the technological process."[60] However,
planning is objected to by the institutional
forces that exist: the status quo of capitalism
supports the invisible hand, not the planner. The
belief is that planning becomes inevitable and
will succeed when the dominance of pecuniary interests gives way to the interests of efficiency and
industrial production. The process is circular
since the technology that created "financial"
dominance in the economy will eventually replace
it with a planning dominance.

It could be argued that technology played a
key role in the emergence of conglomerates because
there has been a revolutionary change in management science since World War II. The catalyst in
this change was the advent of the computer. Managers had been able to introduce computer technology as a tool for use in their decision-making
processes. Mathematical and statistical methodology, once applied only to engineering problems,
had replaced the "seat of the pants" decision-

making in business which had allowed for more efficient control of assets and also for the ability of managers to control more assets efficiently. In addition, today's costs of computers have fallen while the costs of their substitutable input, labor, have increased. Computers allow managers to control effectively more activities. For this reason, firms have the capability to grow and have the incentive to acquire operations that are not advanced in their use of computers. The introduction of further advanced technology could make a profitable firm even more successful. Thus, the rise of conglomerates could be a response to the advent of computer technology and management science.

In addition to the introduction of computer technology, other technological advances have induced diversification. Research and development by firms had grown from $1.5 billion in 1946 to $20 billion in 1968. This research and development spawned new industries--lasers, cyogenics, oceanography, electrooptics, and xerography, as well as new products in plastics, fibers, aircraft, and electronics.[61] As these new products and industries are developed, those that are profitable lead firms into new areas, hence, diversification. Technology may be the one variable most important in explaining the emergence of conglomerates.

Does the emergence of conglomerates portend a planned economy in the future? If financial capitalism is inherently unstable, planning may provide another explanation for the rise of conglomerates. Earnings stability may come about from a firm's ability to practice mutual restraint and cooperation vis-à-vis other firms. If stability results from this evolutionary change in structure, it would reinforce the contemporary structure of capitalism. If, on the other hand, stability is not forthcoming, then conglomerate capitalism will be replaced by a better control mechanism, planning being one possibility.

That stability within the economy is enhanced by the existence of large firms has been suggested by John Kenneth Galbraith.[62] Galbraith believes that the large firm, not the small, is more likely to honor its contractual obligations over the long run since large firms have more control over their economic environment and can sustain unprofitable periods with less difficulty than small firms. The

incentive to control the economic environment
arises because large firms undertake huge investments when deciding to produce a new product or
use a new production process. Given the magnitude
of these changes, the time frame from decision-
making to actual fruition of a new plan is far
from instantaneous. Firms cannot afford the risk
involved in an uncertain market where economic
circumstances may change such that a decision made
in the past may be disastrous in the present.
Firms therefore seek to eliminate market influences
either by vertically integrating and/or by dominating both their markets and their suppliers; thus,
stable market conditions are assured and investment decisions can be implemented. Galbraith has
referred to this as corporate planning.[63]

This corporate planning necessarily involves a
particular type of decision-making organization.
While earlier periods of history had witnessed the
rise of capitalism due to the entrepreneur
(Schumpeter's innovators), Galbraith argues that
the decision-makers today are ordinary men, speci-
alizing in a very narrow field. Through an organizational scheme these men combine their special-
ties into a management team. As Galbraith points
out, "this dispenses with the need for genius"
and at the same time leads to uninspired, but pre-
dictable results.[64] The management group, to borrow a phrase, is the technostructure. Its purpose
is not profit maximization, but instead, the pursuit of firm growth, firm security, and sufficient
earnings to pay for dividends, research and development, and new technology. Thus, Galbraith
assesses corporate management to be a centralized
decision-making body of technically oriented
planners.

As Galbraith has noted, some of the goals of
the technostructure are similar to those of the
government. The premise is that corporations and
government tend to need and use one another. Each
has the same goals of growth, security, and stability and each can achieve these goals only with
the help of the other. It is Galbraith's contention that the achievement of growth, security, and
stability is enhanced by the large size of both
firms and government.

Again, the question that arises is how does
this relate to the evolution of a conglomerate
structure in the economy. Galbraith's analysis of

corporations evolving into security conscious
rather than profit maximizing entities parallels
the security motives discussed in chapter 2. The
multi-product and/or multi-geographical nature of
the firm reduces risk. It may or may not reduce
production cost, but large financial transactions
involve lower costs and give the firm a competitive advantage in receiving loanable funds. Galbraith's theory of the technostructure also fits
with the motive of management security. In addition, control is relevant since conglomerates may
be creating a network of mutual respect and constraint in the marketplace.

It is here that the idea of the technostructure
becomes very interesting. With regard to the nature
of the architects of conglomerates, there is the
question of whether the impetus for diversification stemmed from an individual or a team of managers. If, in general, it is an individual effort,
then Schumpeter's description of a risk-taking
innovator applies. However, if a group of managers
has been responsible for the evolution of conglomerates, then Galbraith's notion of a technostructure is a better label for these decision-makers.
If innovators are responsible, then the market
forces of capitalism are still dominant. If not,
capitalism may have already been replaced by corporate planning groups.

There is the alternative possibility that both
innovators and technocrats have been responsible
for the emergence of conglomerate firms. It is
quite conceivable that the innovators initiated
this form of firm growth, and the technocrats
recognized the merits of this new form of corporate organization and followed suit. The conglomerate merger wave of the 1960s and 1970s may have
evolved in this manner. Of course, this scenario
supports both the Schumpeterian and the Galbraith-
ian postulates regarding firm decision-makers.
Innovators introduce the innovation and cause a
new round of economic activity to start while the
technocrats evaluate this new organizational
structure and determine that they also must diversify or face disadvantages in the marketplace.
Those that adopt the new innovation and diversify
survive this round, those that do not become the
marginal firms of the economy.

Galbraith has pointed to the symbiotic relationship that exists between the large corporations and the government.[65] Cooperation may assure
their mutual survival. While Galbraith has predicted that the industrial system will not long
be regarded as something apart from government,
what is likely to evolve, according to Epstein,
is "an uneasy balance between large and powerful
industrial units and a large and powerful governmental structure with neither partner being ab-
sorbed by the other."[66] Logically, then, firms
would continue to seek political power. William
Kornhauser has suggested that this positively
reinforces the economic/political system. Significant involvement in politics necessarily means
that firms have just as much at stake in maintaining the stability of the system as does the government.[67] The Lockheed bailout is often cited as a
manifestation of the symbiotic relationship between government and large firms; the recent
Chrysler bailout provides another example. Should
bankruptcy of such large firms be permitted, the
economic consequences would be severe. That government rescues major, private enterprises lends credence to Epstein's phrase "uneasy balance" and
further supports not only the postulates regarding
cooperation between government and business but
also the various arguments of economic power, conglomerate power, and political power.

The emergence of conglomerates suggests various
kinds of scenarios that are possible as evolutionary paths for our capitalistic system. There are
at least three clear alternatives: capitalism is
continuing to be dominated by a few firms--con-
glomerates being the latest dominant structure;
capitalism is moving into a transitory phase which
precedes socialism (government ownership of the
means of production); or capitalism is giving way
to a corporate planning system (private ownership
of the means of production and planning within the
economy by large, private firms). As to which of
these scenarios actually is forthcoming depends on
the actors that are responsible for a conglomerate
market structure, the technology, the needs of the
collective society for stability and security, and
the actual goals of the corporations. I shall
focus on these possible evolutionary paths and try
to ascertain in which of these directions the

emergence of a conglomerate structure seems to be moving our economic system.

I begin with the view that the rise of conglomerates may essentially be just a new form of monopoly capitalism. Conglomerate organization may be an innovation that leads the capitalistic economy to a new round of growth and expansion. If this is correct, then one would have to conclude that capitalism, as an economic system, is not threatened at this time.

Further, conglomerate arrangements do facilitate and encourage financial manipulations and can be construed as supportive for a system that values financial results over physical output. Conglomerates may be neither new nor different from the trusts that evolved at the turn of the last century. This conclusion also reinforces the premise that the status of capitalism is enhanced, not threatened, by the evolution of conglomerate firms.

Finally, it is conceivable that conglomerates are a more powerful class of interest groups for, diversified corporations may be capable of generating more power over the decision-making processes within the economy than a firm which produces a single-product or operates in a single geographical area. In this vein, the increased success of firms as interest groups also would be supportive of the argument that our system was evolving along the path of competitive capitalism.

The second evolutionary path leads to the public ownership of the means of production. Here the argument would be that a conglomerate structure is incompatible with economic growth and stability. Both the increase in the centralization of the means of production and the decrease in the number of decision-makers in the economy threaten the competitive climate so necessary for growth and development. Also the possibility of a bankruptcy occurring by one or among a group of these giant firms threatens the stability of the system. The elimination of growth or stability or both in the economic system would bring ever increasing pressure on the government to intervene and take over the responsibility of allocating our resources.

The third evolutionary path leads to corporate planning. While one of the basic tenets of capitalism is consumer sovereignty (suppliers adjust the quantity and quality of their products to the demands of consumers), it has been argued that

modern capitalism is really a euphemism for producer sovereignty (consumers adjust to the quantity
and quality of the products offered by producers).
Here firms determine the allocation of resources
and do so through long range planning. Conglomerate
firms may be a more efficient structure for con-
trolling the economy. By having the largest firms
create a network of interaction, respect, restraint,
and interdependence, the accomplishment of successful planning can be assured. Since conglomerates
become viable structures for planning given modern
advances in technology, their existence makes control of the economy that much easier. Thus, conglomerates may be taking us to a new round of capitalist expansion, or leading us down the road to
government control, or carrying us to a more entrenched and solidified base of corporate planning.

Does the evolution of a conglomerate structure
bring with it a more or less stable and healthy
economic environment? Obviously, society cannot
survive without a stable and healthy economy, so
the decisions made by government and business must
lend themselves to supporting economic structures
that lead to the assurance of stability and security. The competitive markets of Jeffersonian capitalism have a great deal of uncertainty and risk
implicit in their working. Perhaps this uncertainty led to the drive for monopoly status by firms.
Also, perhaps government allowed this transition
because of its own needs and desires for the elimination of uncertainty and risk in the marketplace.
If these arguments are correct, then the evolution
of conglomerates would be more evidence of such
values. More control by firms over the economic
and political environments reduces uncertainty and
risk. Perhaps this is the key that unlocks the
answer. The various actors in our society may want
corporate and/or political power to evolve for
their own security, and corporations and government may be responding to these inherent values of
our system. The end result is that all get what
they want as fewer, more diversified firms dominate the economy and the political process.

A summary of the major points of this chapter
are included in Figure 5.1 below. This figure dis-
plays the evolutionary path capitalism has taken
over the past years and indicates the possible
evolutionary paths conglomerate capitalism may
take the economy in the future.

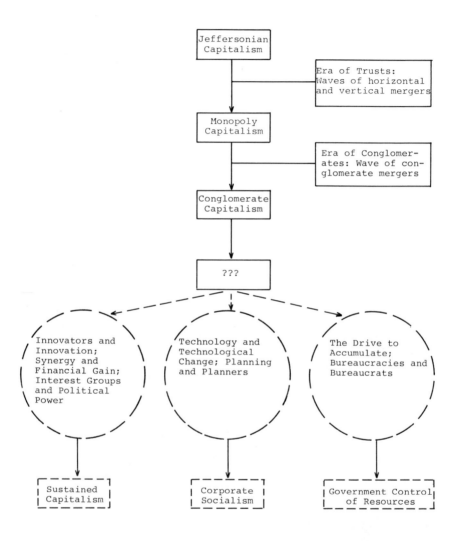

Fig. 5.1. The evolution of capitalism

6 Conglomerates and Policy

THERE is little argument that government should intervene when markets wander too far from the competitive ideal. Even Adam Smith, who championed competition and laissez faire economics, supported government intervention under certain circumstances. The debate today regarding government policy in a particular noncompetitive market concerns the policies that are to be implemented. Viable policies include tax incentives, price controls, tariffs and quotas, regulation, public ownership, or antitrust enforcement. Each noncompetitive situation which calls for a policy decision is unique; therefore, the policy must also be unique and especially fitted to the situation. The following discussion concentrates on the problematic nature of the debate with respect to the emergence of conglomerates and the policy alternatives the government has considered in dealing with these firms. The government has been neither clear nor consistent regarding its policies in this area. Indeed, the government's behavior may reflect the absence of a clear and concise economic theory upon which to base its policy.

A competitive market structure is preferred because of the benefits it bestows on society. Also, costs and prices are minimized while output is maximized, thus allowing for the maximum amount of employment and the most efficient use of resources. Whenever elements exist in a market to prohibit competition, the market is said to be imperfectly competitive. Higher prices and lower output are the results of such a market. It is in these imperfectly competitive markets that policy measures are required. Without opting for one of the policy tools, society is trading off the benefits of lower prices, higher output, maximum employment, and the efficient use of resources that are derived from more competitive markets.

The theories advanced by economists concerning the effect of conglomerates on competition are divided according to whether they have a micro or macro orientation. The micro approach is narrow, focusing on the potential benefit or harm that may accrue to a relevant market given the entrance of a conglomerate. The macro approach takes a broader perspective, viewing the potential effects of the emergence of large diversified firms on the competitive nature of the economic system.

There are two alternative routes a firm may follow in its attempt to diversify: the firm may choose to enter a new market de novo, or it may acquire (merge with) an existing firm in a new market. The difference between the approaches is that de novo diversification increases the number of competitors in a market; merging does not. Also, when a merger takes place, the acquired firm becomes transformed, for it now is a component part of a large enterprise. The merger approach has been more popular because it is quicker and because it reduces the degree of uncertainty relative to de novo. When considering the policy implications conglomerate mergers pose regarding market structure, micro economists focus on whether the nature of the entry will have a positive or negative effect on competition in that market.

We have already noted that Mueller believes that conglomerate firms are "capturing the commanding market shares in the highly concentrated, highly differentiated oligopolies." of the economy. John Narver has analyzed the possible effects of mergers in markets where highly concentrated and/or highly differentiated oligopolies exist.[1] He concluded that competition will be harmed in those instances where a large, conglomerate firm acquires

1. A firm that is large in an already highly concentrated market.
2. A firm with product differentiation and differentiation is a substantial barrier.
3. A firm that has common points of production and distribution with the conglomerate in a market with moderate to high scale economy barriers.[2]

On the other hand, he suggested that competition may be enhanced when a large, conglomerate firm acquires a relatively small firm in an oligopolistic industry.[3] The power of the acquiring firm could help the acquiree take customers away from the larger, established firms. This is known as the toehold theory. When a conglomerate acquires a relatively small firm in a concentrated market, it has established a "beachhead" (toehold) in that industry. Growing would require introducing competition in the industry, thus reducing the control the larger firms have on the market. Narver's point is that the nature of the merger must be considered because there are instances where competition could be harmed but others where it might be enhanced.

Donald Turner, head of the Antitrust Division of the Justice Department during the early and middle 1960s, set down three structural guidelines to be used in determining whether conglomerate merger activity is harmful to competition. When a potential competitor acquires a firm in a market where one, the market is oligopolistic in nature; two, the acquiring firm is a very likely entrant to this market; and three, the acquiring firm could be a de novo entrant, the merger is likely to exert harmful effects on competition.[4] Turner's first requirement conforms to the positions of both Narver and Mueller. All agree that the degree of concentration in a market is a parameter that must be considered. But one must note the problem inherent in the second and third guidelines.

The second guideline is difficult to deal with since conglomerates, by definition, are potential entrants in many markets; therefore it would be difficult not to consider them likely candidates in a particular market. The obvious difficulties not withstanding, there has been support for this second guideline. The argument is that one could consider conglomerate mergers somewhat distant from but related to vertical mergers.[5] Granted, the tie between the markets of a conglomerate merger is weak or nonexistant; however, the fact that the merger occurs indicates that ties exist, whether obvious or not. Whenever such ties do exist, a conglomerate firm must be considered a likely entrant. The only difference between a conglomerate and vertical merger, in this context, is

that conglomerates are less likely, but not un-
likely to enter a market.

Regarding the third condition, conglomerates,
by their nature to date, tend to acquire firms
rather than enter markets de novo. The preference
for acquisition seems to make the third guideline
difficult to follow because there is a significant
difference between "could" and "would." The argument could be made by a firm that it could enter
a market de novo, but that it probably would enter
through acquisition or not at all.

Under what conditions should we expect competition to be lessened due to conglomerate mergers in
oligopoly markets? Peter O. Steiner points out
that when entry is made into an already tight
oligopoly market, the conglomerate may be able to
create some competition where none existed, particularly if the tight oligopoly contains ineffi-
ciencies. Certainly, if the oligopoly market has
vigorous competition, then nothing can be gained
and much can be lost if the merger is allowed.[6]
Probably the strongest statement that micro economists would make is this: in those instances
where a tight, inefficient oligopoly exists and a
conglomerate acquires a toehold in that market,
competition might be enhances; otherwise, a merger
probably will not enhance competition and may even
lessen it.

Charles Berry has done empirical work in this
area. He has tested the hypothesis regarding the
question of whether conglomerate activity is harmful to competition. In 1975, he pointed out that
"for large firms, the conventional route to entry
or diversification is the corporate acquisition or
merger," so he focused his attention on acquisitions by the largest manufacturing firms in the
economy (461 firms).[7] He first tested the hypothesis that entry by a conglomerate into a market via
acquisition tended to increase the 4-firm, 4-digit
concentration ratio. His results suggest that this
hypothesis is unfounded: "Where concentration was
initially high, the rate of entry by firms among
this group of large corporations was positively
and significantly associated with decreasing 4-
firm, 4-digit concentration."[8] This supports certain views (toehold and inefficient oligopolies)
which hold that under certain circumstances competition may be enhanced by conglomerate entry into
a market.

Berry's tests have also shown that

> There is a negative association between
> change in the share of the four (or eight)
> largest sellers in concentrated industries
> and entry by large firms. Not only that,
> but the regression results suggest the mir-
> ror image in the case of entry by small
> firms--where concentration is high, entry
> by small firms appears to make no signifi-
> cant effect on a reduction in industry
> concentration.

> That is the most worrisome (and perhaps
> also the most interesting) result--rela-
> tively strong evidence that the market
> position of leading firms _is_ protected in
> concentrated industries from entry by other
> than large firms.[9]

It appears that entry by large firms can increase
competition in concentrated markets while entry by
smaller firms may not. Prohibiting large firms
from entering concentrated markets, and encouraging smaller firms instead, could be misguided
policy.

What impact does this have on the theoretical
conclusions? Narver concluded that in highly concentrated industries a conglomerate acquiring a
large firm would probably lessen competition but
possibly may enhance it. Berry found that only the
entry by large firms increases competition. In
addition, he found that a smaller firm's entrance
has no effect on concentration. Narver argued that
smaller firms would have the greatest effect when
acquired by a large conglomerate. This may support
Berry's first conclusion, but both Berry and Narver
are essentially arguing that unless the "new firm,"
that is, the acquiree and the acquiror, is large,
there will be no positive effect on competition.

In a micro sense, these theories point to one
of the policy dilemmas facing the government today.
It is not clear that conglomerate mergers in concentrated markets harm competition. Oliver Williamson has stated the case concisely: "An understanding of the conglomerate phenomenon is impeded if
all conglomerates are treated as though they were
indistinguishable one from another. Some types may
pose genuine public policy problems, others have

an invigorating competitive influence, and still others have had neutral effects."[10]

The macro approach concerns itself with the effect on competition, not only in the relevant market the conglomerate enters, but also on the competitive nature of the economic system as a whole. One finds arguments based on the anticompetitive nature of conglomerate power itself and on the degree of increasing aggregate concentration caused by conglomerate mergers. John M. Blair and Walter Adams, as well as Mueller, have suggested that in any market which a large, conglomerate firm enters, competition is automatically retarded.[11] Smaller competitors will not challenge the power of the conglomerate, nor will potential competitors be as likely to enter if they will have to face such a formidable foe.

The emergence of a set of conglomerate firms in the economy increases aggregate concentration by definition, and puts in place an aggregate market structure which encourages conduct not unlike that of Edward's spheres of influence hypothesis.[12] This hypothesis holds that large, diversified firms would meet each other in many different markets and would come to realize the gains that could accrue to them through interdependent behavior and competitive forbearance. If this type of economic structure gives firms the incentive to behave in such a manner, one should pause before defending conglomerate mergers.

The macro approach goes beyond market considerations and addresses the implications of conglomerate power in the political arena. Large, diversified firms have many resources at their command and have the discretionary power to use them as desired. Since the evidence indicates that large firms are more active in the political arena than small firms, macro theorists suspect that conglomerate power can yield undue influence in government.[13] The macro position is clear: conglomerates are undesirable because of the power they possess due to sheer size and diversification. This power is harmful to competition--both broadly and narrowly defined--because it increases aggregate concentration; increases opportunities for cross-subsidization and reciprocity; increases barriers to entry; dampens the incentive of potential competitors; blunts the competitive drive of firms by creating a network of markets which allows for mutual forbearance; and finally, threatens to undermine the democratic nature of our political system.

The Congress and the courts have had to weigh the merits of the micro as well as the macro approaches in making their decisions regarding conglomerates. The micro and macro approaches are, on occasion, in opposition to one another; at other times they simply address different concerns. Government representatives have vacillated between the two, sometimes approaching conglomerates from a narrow, micro perspective and at other times taking the broad, macro view.

Regarding conglomerates, the government's policies have not been very clear or consistent over the last two decades. Since the effect of conglomerate activity on the economy is uncertain, Congress had been reluctant to pass any laws to specifically deal with conglomerates and market structure. What has evolved is a mix of policies (sometimes by the same administrator in different years) and efforts at prosecution.

Concern about conglomerate mergers and conglomerates in general has been elevated since the late 1950s when the frequency of conglomerate mergers started rising. Until that time, most antitrust policy had been directed at horizontal and vertical mergers, and the emphasis was primarily on the maintenance of the number of competitors in markets when there was a demonstrated attempt to reduce that number through merger. When questions arose regarding conglomerate mergers and the existence of conglomerate firms, the Antitrust Division initially argued that conglomerate activities were not within the purview of the Justice Department. Those who argued that conglomerate activity should be considered cited Section 7 of the Clayton Act for grounds. Nevertheless, Turner, head of the Antitrust Division, "made it clear both before he took office and after, that in his view the conglomerate merger (except in well-defined situations) did not (and should not) come under the general antitrust determinents of Section 7."[14] Turner argued that the Congress should pass legislation in this area before the Justice Department could prosecute conglomerate mergers and/or bigness.

As Figure 6.1 shows, there was, between 1965 and 1968, an accelerated rate of increase in the

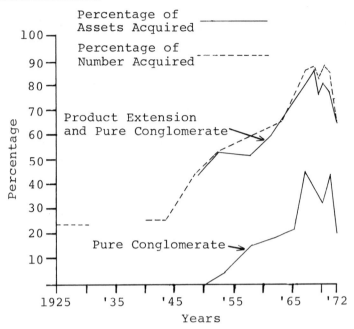

Fig. 6.1. Large conglomerate mergers as a percentage of all large mergers

SOURCE: Figs. 1-6, Steiner, Mergers (Ann Arbor: Univ. of Michigan Press, 1975), p. 22.

amount of conglomerate mergers taking place, the likes of which had not been previously experienced. In 1968, Turner, still head of the Antitrust Division, reversed his previous position. One can only speculate that the policy reversal was prompted by the high degree of merger activity. The Justice Department issued guidelines (just before Turner's service ended) regarding conglomerates.

> they (the guidelines) attempt to extend it (coverage by Clayton Act, Sec. 7) to conglomerate mergers using the potential competition, reciprocity, and entrenchment arguments developed (in previous cases) . . . they (the guidelines) came close to being per se rules against conglomerate mergers that met certain structural standards (large firms-large firm mergers)[15]

The argument of potential competition, referring to the possibility of firms entering a particular market, has been used successfully in antitrust cases involving both vertical and horizontal mergers. When a firm decides to integrate itself upstream or downstream, it has the choice of either acquiring a firm that operates in one of those markets or entering the market de novo. Recall that, in either case, the firm gains entry into a new market. If there is a merger, there will be the same number of firms afterwards; de novo diversification means that there will be one more. The policy of the Justice Department has been to prohibit a merger when the acquirer could be considered a potential entrant into the market. Circumstances such as these have led the courts to support the argument of potential competition. A classic example is found in the 1964, El Paso Natural Gas Case.[16] El Paso, a Texas natural gas company, acquired Pacific Northwest Pipeline Co., also a natural gas company. The two firms had not actually met in any markets but the potential for competition was there. Actually, El Paso supplied gas to the California market, and Pacific Northwest wanted to do likewise but had not yet been successful in its attempts. Since Pacific Northwest was a potential competitor (although not an actual competitor) of El Paso, the Supreme Court ruled in this case that potential competition is no less an amount of competition and disallowed the merger.

Regarding conglomerate mergers, potential competition has been used by the Justice Department as a basis for attempting to deny mergers. Ironically, one of the most cogent statements regarding the applicability of the concept of potential competition was made by James Rahl. It is ironic because Rahl was actually pointing out his belief in the illegitimacy of this theory when he made the following statement:

> It (acquiring firm) had a choice of two methods of achieving entry--to acquire an existing firm, or to build its own new facilities. Its decision to enter by acquisition has resulted in a loss of an opportunity to increase competition in the industry. Therefore, it may be argued, the acquisition has lessened competition. The competition lessened is competition which did not exist, but which was "potential" in the

sense that it is competition which the firm
in question might have created itself.[17]

Reciprocity is also given consideration as a
reason for disallowing conglomerate mergers. Recall from Chapter 2 that reciprocity occurs when
firms exchange economic agreements, and conglomerates, by their very nature, are candidates for
reciprocal dealings. By being multi-product firms,
they compete with many firms over a broad range of
products. It follows, then, that the possibilities
for reciprocal arrangements are enhanced. Thus,
the imperfect competition which results from agreements that foreclose markets makes this aspect of
conglomerate mergers undesirable.
When an acquired firm becomes economically
secure by becoming a part of a giant conglomerate,
it immediately has access to the economic power of
the large conglomerate and increases its probability of becoming entrenched in the marketplace.
There are at least two anticompetitive results
that are possible. First, the smaller firm might
occupy a superior position vis-à-vis any potential
entrant and would thereby dispel any notion of
entry by potential competitors. Second, if the
acquired firm had been serving a market with low
concentration, the competitive balance would be
upset and a lessening of competition would result.
In 1968, the Antitrust Division of the Justice
Department had agreed to prosecute conglomerate
activity when it involved lessening competition.
Measurements of a lessening of competition would
be based on the loss of potential competition, the
practice of reciprocity, and the degree of en-
trenchment afforded. However, 1968 was also the
year that President Johnson left office and President Nixon was elected. While President Johnson
was still in office and Nixon was President-elect,
both announced that they were appointing task
forces to look into the conglomerate activity in
the economy. These task forces were to evaluate
the effects of conglomerates on competition and
then recommend appropriate policy measures.
President Johnson's Task Force on Antitrust
Policy was directed by Phil Neal, dean of the
Chicago Law School. The Task Force noted that "the
current rate and pattern of (conglomerate) mergers
is causing significant and apparently permanent
changes in the structure of the economy, and the

long-run impact of these changes cannot be readily
foreseen."[18] Objections to these mergers were made
by the Task Force on the grounds that they have an
adverse effect on competitive structure and behavior in certain markets, and that the increase
aggregate concentration and thereby decrease the
number of decision-making units in the economy.[19]
The Task Force felt that competition could be enhanced if merger activity could be directed toward
smaller firms because the larger firm could help
the smaller firm increase its share of the market
(the toehold theory). If the toehold policy could
not be implemented, then the only encouragement
should be for large conglomerates to diversify de
novo.[20] To this end, the Neal Report recommended
the passage of a new statute, The Merger Act,
which would prohibit any large firm from merging
with any "leading firm" in a particular industry.
A large firm was defined as one with assets over
$250 million or sales over $500 million.[21] A leading firm, by definition, was one of the top four
in a market in which the four largest accounted
for at least 50% of total sales. The market would
have to have sales exceeding $100 million and the
firm in question would have to have at least a 10%
share.[22]

President-elect Nixon's Task Force was headed
by George Stigler. Observing the very same merger
activity, this Task Force came to radically different conclusions and did not view conglomerate
mergers as a threat to competition. It suggested
that more harm than good could come to the economy
by not allowing a free flow of activity in the
marketplace. It recommended that the government
follow a passive policy. "We seriously doubt that
the Antitrust Division should embark upon an
active program of challenging conglomerate enterprises on the basis of nebulous fears about size
and economic power. These fears should be either
confirmed or disipated. . . . Vigorous action on
the basis of our present knowledge is not defen-
sible."[23]

Reid evaluated the reports of the two Task
Forces. He noted that the Stigler Report virtually
ignored the conglomerate movement, while the Neal
Report was a thorough, relevant, specific, and
helpful document.[24] Stigler, himself, had argued
some twenty years earlier that economists of the
early 1900s had been remiss in their view toward

the merger wave of that era.[25] He had charged
economists with considering these mergers to be
natural events. They (economists) were not
"bothered that . . . economies of scale should
spring forth suddenly and simultaneously in an
enormous variety of industries and yet pass over
the minor firms that characteristically persisted
and indeed flourished in those industries."[26]
Mueller has pointed out the irony of Stigler's
past and current positions:

> Future historians will almost certainly find
> it incomprehensible that the Stigler Group,
> deliberating at the very moment when mergers
> reached a new all-time national record, ex-
> pressed no concern with that accelerating
> conglomerate merger movement and treated the
> arguments that conglomerate mergers often
> eliminate potential competition or result
> in anti-competitive reciprocity opportunities
> as largely "makeweights."[27]

Consistent with Turner's initial position, in
the period 1965-1968, the Antitrust Division
focused on vertical and horizontal mergers rather
than conglomerate. Nonetheless, some of the mergers that the Department sought to deny during
this period did have conglomerate characteristics.
In the Consolidated Foods/Gentry and General
Dynamics/Liquid Carbonic proposed mergers, reciprocity had been a major factor in the delibera-
tions. The decision in each case was to disallow
the merger. Proctor & Gamble and Clorox were not
permitted to merge on the grounds that barriers to
entry would be created and that potential competition of Proctor & Gamble with Clorox would be
eliminated. In the case of General Foods and SOS,
the court relied on the principle of potential
competition.[28] Even though it was not at all probable that General Foods, a producer of packaged
food, would be a potential competitor of SOS, a
maker of soap pads, the court felt that the principle should still apply. Thus, through 1967 the
courts supported the Justice Department's prosecution of conglomerate-related mergers on the
grounds of reciprocity and potential competition.
   At the beginning of President Nixon's tenure in
office, the expectations for conglomerate merger
prosecutions were quite low. The Stigler Task

Force, appointed by Nixon, had made its position quite clear. Ironically, Richard McLaren, whom Nixon appointed to replace Turner as head of the Antitrust Division, held opinions which largely reflected Turner's guidelines. After his appointment was made, McLaren ruled that conglomerate mergers were anticompetitive. He argued that Section 7 of the Clayton Act was broad enough to include conglomerate mergers, and promptly set out to prosecute them.[29] As the following cases demonstrate, the prosecution was based for the most part on reciprocity and to a lesser extent on potential competition.

In 1969, cases were brought against five conglomerate mergers. The attempt to prohibit Ling-Temco-Vought's (LTV) acquisition of Jones and Laughlin Steel was settled out of court.[30] LTV was in financial difficulty and a consent decree was filed to allow reorganization. In the case of the Northwest Industries merger with B.F. Goodrich, a district court found reciprocity to be a weak argument and did not stand in Northwest's way.[31] Three cases were brought against mergers involving ITT: one with Hartford Insurance, another with Grinnell Corporation, and a third with Canteen Corporation.[32] The fact that ITT was a large conglomerate, and Hartford a large insurance company with substantial earnings and cash flow, made this a strategic case. It could have become the case which would have determined the status of conglomerate mergers for years to come. The Justice Department worked two years in its preparation, but the case was never tried because an out of court settlement was arranged by means of a consent decree. The decree allowed ITT to keep Hartford Insurance if it (ITT) would divest itself of four of its other subsidiaries and agree not to acquire any firms with assets exceeding $100 million over the next ten years.[33] ITT chose to divest itself of both Grinnell Corporation and Canteen Corporation.

Two comments are in order here. First, not one of these five cases ever reached the Supreme Court. The reason could not be because of a hostile court as the Justice Department has had a virtually perfect record of success in merger cases it had appealed to the Supreme Court since 1950.[34] Second, in the ITT-Hartford case, McLaren himself acknowledged that he "missed a shot at a landmark

decision."[35] He defended his decision to agree to
a consent decree because it was in the best interest of the economy.[36] Apparently the Justice
Department felt itself to be best qualified to
serve as prosecutor, judge, and jury in this
instance. The ITT/Hartford merger was a clear cut
case involving a large, conglomerate merging with
a dominant firm in an unrelated industry. The loss
of an opportunity to test this merger in the
courts is immeasurable.

While McLaren relied primarily on reciprocity
in these five cases, potential competition played
a major role in several others. The Court's opinion, handed down in three key cases during 1971 to
1973, indicates its acceptance of potential competition as a viable weapon in disallowing conglomerate mergers. In 1961, Ford Motor Company acquired
Autolite, a maker of spark plugs.[37] Autolite, with
12% of the market, competed primarily with Champion
and AC owned by General Motors). Ford acknowledged
that it could have entered de novo but that would
have taken too long. The District Court and the
Supreme Court argued that Ford would be a more
useful competitor in this market by entering de
novo or by remaining a potential competitor,
thereby serving as a deterrent to the existing
firms in the market. Thus, Ford was considered
more useful as a potential competitor than as an
actual competitor or as a de novo entrant than as
an acquiror.

When Bendix, a large aerospace and engineering
firm, acquired Fram, a large automobile oil filter
firm, the FTC charged that this was anticompetitive due to the size of Bendix and the share of
the oil filter market held by Fram.[38] The FTC
pointed out that Bendix had three choices if it
wanted to enter the oil filter market: de novo
entry, toehold entry, or merger with a leading
firm. By choosing either de novo or toehold entry,
Bendix would become a competitor of Fram. This
would increase competition, something which certainly is acceptable under Section 7. The merger
between the two would mean that Bendix and Fram
would become one firm, the number of competitors
in the oil filter market would not change, but now
one of the firms would be substantially larger.
Ultimately, this would lessen competition. The
entry of Bendix into this market was not chal-
lenged, the nature of that entry was.

The issue of geographical diversification was considered in Falstaff Brewing Corporation's acquisition of Narrangansett Brewing.[39] Falstaff was the fourth largest New England brewer, and its stated position was that it did not wish to enter the New England market except through acquisition. The District Court found that Falstaff was not a potential competitor in the New England market, but the Supreme Court was not impressed and cited several reasons for sending the case back for reconsideration. First, a competitor on the fringe is no less a competitor even if entrance is not contemplated de novo. Firms already in the market would consider the fringe firm a potential entrant and adjust their behavior accordingly. Second, even though Falstaff indicated that it would enter only through acquisition, this was not necessarily a long-run decision. Circumstances would change in the future, enticing Falstaff to enter de novo.

The positions taken by the courts and the FTC in these three cases indicate support for the idea of potential competition. Steiner has observed that

It now seems that the courts are willing to invoke Section 7 against an acquisition if competition is adversely affected by any one of: elimination of a probable de novo entrant, elimination of a threat on the edge of the market, replacement of a powerful threat on the edge of the market by a beefed-up competitor in the industry (the doctrine of Ford-Autolite), entry via acquisition of a leading producer rather than by an available smaller one, and an entry that increases the subsequent barriers to entry for other potential entrants. At least in terms of competitive effects this seems a sufficient arsenal with which to shoot down any merger that poses any threat to competition.[40]

Future attitudes of the Courts, the Justice Department, and the FTC will play an important role in determining how effective Section 7 will be. An equally important role will be played by the firms themselves. The higher the frequency of conglomerate mergers, the more forceful will be the positions of the Courts, the Justice, and the FTC.

Senator Edward Kennedy has recently submitted a

bill to prohibit mergers by large firms.[41] His
plan is very similar to the proposed Merger Act
that the Neal Task Force recommended some ten years
ago. Mergers would be illegal between firms having
$2.5 billion of sales or $2 billion of assets.
Firms having over $350 million of sales or $200
million of assets would have to justify merger on
an economic basis. Mergers between firms with more
than $100 million of assets would also have to be
justified if the combined assets of the merging
firms exceeds $1 billion.[42] It would appear that
the rationale for this bill lies in the fact that
conglomerate merger activity between large firms,
which had slowed in the early 1970s, picked up
speed in the late 1970s. Figure 6.2 demonstrates
this point.

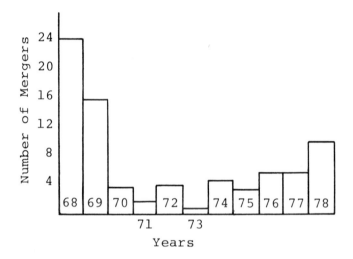

Fig. 6.2. Mergers between Fortune 500 firms

SOURCE: Fortune Magazine, "The Biggest Buying
Spree Since the Sixties," May 7, 1979, p. 306.

It would seem that Senator Kennedy is seeking to
stem the tide of the new merger wave. He has drawn
support for his proposal from both the Justice
Department and the FTC; however, unanimous support
is not forthcoming from the academic community.
Yale Brozen, Harold Demsetz, and Fred Weston have
attacked the bill as pernicious. They feel that
the evidence does not support the position that
bigness is anticompetitive. Indeed, their research

suggest that large, diversified firms create a competitive environment in the economy. Brozen has argued that the relationship between concentration and rate of return is weak which supports the view that concentrated industries are competitive.[43] Demetz found a strong positive relationship between firm size and rate of return which suggests that growth enhances the well-being of the firm and therefore should not be denied.[44] Weston tracked the rate of inflation in an array of industries between 1967 and 1977 and found a negative correlation between concentration and inflation.[45]

This debate should sound familiar for the Kennedy proposal falls on the side of the Neal Task Force while the dissent of Brozen, Demsetz, and Weston is supportive of the Stigler Task Force. The same battle is still being fought, and each side has produced more data to strengthen its position. If conglomerate mergers continue to increase in frequency, one can rest assured that each side will work even harder to prove that their position is correct.

As some economists have noted, "Policies are what 'Policy Makers' do. They are not chiselled in stone nor decreed from on high."[46] The idea is to identify problematic areas where power (market, economic, or conglomerate) exists and try to ascertain whether this power is detrimental to the competitive process. If it is, then the policy makers must choose an appropriate measure to abrogate that power.

Micro oriented economists believe that the entry of a conglomerate firm into a market could either enhance, harm, or leave unchanged the competitive nature of that market. The actual outcome will be a function of the degree of concentration in the market, the size of the conglomerate and the firm acquired, and the competitive tactics used. If policy makers subscribe to a micro approach, then their evaluation will be done on a case by case basis. There will be no uniform set of guidelines or per se rules. Each conglomerate merger case will be settled on its own merits.

To macro oriented economists, the matter is much less complicated: bigness is harmful to our competitive system per se and bigness coupled with extensive diversification is doubly harmful. Should policy makers follow the macro approach exclusively, the measures would be quite clear:

disallow all mergers between firms of a certain
size, disallow four firm concentration to reach a
particular level in any market, and disallow any
firm from having a disproportionate share of any
market. This policy would reduce, if not eliminate,
all facets of power in the system.

The predominant policy positions regarding conglomerates have been based on the micro approach,
so the focus has generally been on the effect the
conglomerate will have on competition in the market that it is entering. While there has always
been support for the macro approach, per se rules
have not been legislated and, when formulated
into guidelines by the Justice Department, do not
hold up to the test of time.

That policy makers have vacillated in their
position regarding conglomerates is a function of
the above mentioned opposing and often different
views held by economists. It would seem that policy in the future will depend on the activity of
conglomerates. Should another wave of mergers similar to the late 1960s develop, as the data in
1978 and 1979 suggests, then the macro approach
will probably gain supporters. Otherwise, the
micro approach of a case by case policy will
dominate.

In the 1960s the economy was burgeoning. Established markets were expanding and new markets were
opening. Concurrent with this robust economic
activity, economists held the optimistic belief
that economic theory was so sufficiently sophisticated that the economy could be fine-tuned. If
there was any doubt, it was dispelled when President Kennedy's tax cut propelled the economy
toward full employment in the early 1960s just as
the theory has predicted. Capitalizing on the
euphoria which prevailed and the momentum of the
economy, businessmen set about to expand their
economic activities. It became evident very early
in this growth oriented era that acquisition (diversification) provided the fast track.

In the late 1960s the economy lost its vitality.
The inflationary pressures resulting from the
Vietnam War called for governmental policies of
restraint and an economic slowdown followed.
Growth through acquisition diminished as the slowdown worked its way through the economy. The opti-
mism of economists regarding the viability of fine-
tuning gave way to pessimism and cynicism since

the new policy measures could not control inflation and managed to increase unemployment as well.
During the digestive phase of this slowdown, an
obscure cartel, OPEC, emerged as a dominant economic force. The significant increases in oil
prices that it imposed further exacerbated the
pressures on inflation and unemployment. The
1970s have been troubled and difficult to an
extent which would never have been predicted in
the blossoming period of the early and mid 1960s.

Although firm diversification slowed with the
economy in the early 1970s, the lethargy was not
sustained in the late 1970s. Diversification began
to increase. This time, however, it was different
than that which had occurred in the 1960s when the
catch phrases had been "go-go stocks," entrepre-
neurial ego trips, and synergy. In the late seven-
ties the tone was different. There was no razzle-
dazzle, no glamour (with the exception of the
publicity generated from hostile takeovers, of
course) because firms diversified for security.
Growth itself projects the image of a healthy
firm, while growth through diversification allows
for preferential treatment in the market for loanable funds, a reduction in earning's risk, and an
assurance to managers for a secure future.

It seems that the diversifying efforts of large
firms continue independent of the robustness of
the economy. Indeed, good times seem to buoy
acquisitions while bad times seem to require them.
Steiner has observed that the conglomerate mergers
of the 1960s represented a wave that peaked and
eventually crashed.

> How will the conglomerate merger wave of the
> 1960's look from the perspective of the year
> 2000? My guess is that to the historians it
> will be regarded from that vantage point as
> an interesting episode, somewhat more impor-
> tant (in its long-run effects) that the
> Florida land boom, and somewhat less conse-
> quential than the 1937 depression. Perhaps,
> like the NRA, it will be regarded as an
> episode that threatened to achieve a last-
> ing transformation of the industrial land-
> scape, but failed to do so.[47]

Given the evidence of an increase in conglomerate activity in the late 1970s, coupled with the

continued diversification indicated by the data in Chapter 3, growth through diversification <u>should</u> be expected to continue in the future. This will certainly result in a profound structural transformation of the economy.

It seems that with continued diversification, the old measures and theories used to evaluate individual markets and competition will give way to new measures. For instance, it is logical to expect the traditional theories that focus on market share and market concentration to decline in emphasis and be replaced by theories regarding aggregate share and aggregate concentration. In addition, there will be a need for more emphasis on developing indices that measure economic, conglomerate, and political power. The system has become too complex and interrelated to do otherwise.

Appendixes

APPENDIX A

A Case Study of a Union's Experience with Litton Industries

LITTON Industries is a diversified manufacturing firm. In 1969, its business activities encompassed seventeen separate products in four unrelated product groups. There was a great deal of balance within these product areas as no one of them accounted for more than 13% of the firm's sales. One product that the firm manufactures is typewriters, specifically, Royal brand typewriters. Litton acquired the Royal firm and its multi-plant operation. In addition, it acquired several overseas producers of typewriters, Triumph-Adler being one of these.

   The negotiations over a new collective bargaining contract at the Springfield, Missouri plant of Royal broke down in 1969, and the union went on strike. Litton closed down the plant and the local management indicated that the central management committee of Litton had made this decision. The local union was not in a position to bargain with anyone other than the local management. In addition, Litton sent part of the work being done in Springfield to its Hartford plant and the rest overseas. So, the conglomerate nature of Litton allowed it to thwart a local union at the bargaining table without bearing any economic consequences itself. In fact, a few days before the strike vote, "the plant manager delivered a cafeteria speech in which he advised against attending the union meeting. He warned that a strike would only invite relocation of production abroad. Litton has typewriter plants at its disposal in Germany, Japan, Holland, England as well as Hartford, Conn." This experience by the union in Springfield, Missouri, is a clear indication of the bargaining power possessed by a conglomerate firm. It is also clear that for unions to achieve equal power they must be able to meet firms like Litton with a

This information was drawn from "Collective Bargaining in the Conglomerate, Multinational Firm: Litton's Shutdown of Royal Typewriter," Charles Craypo, _Industrial_ _and_ _Labor_ _Relations_ _Review_, Vol. 29, Number 1, Oct., 1975.

united front representing all the employees a conglomerate firm employs.

APPENDIX B

A Case Study of General Electric and Coalition
Bargaining, 1965-1970

IN 1966, General Electric (G. E.) had bargaining
agreements with 14 international unions. The 14
unions represented 181 locals and 132,685 of
G. E.'s employees. (See Table B.1, below.) Historically, G. E. bargained with these international
unions individually. In 1965, six of the unions
decided that a joint effort should be undertaken
in the 1966 negotiations; they issued the following statement: "Just as American labor down through
the years found that it is futile for individuals
to try to bargain with large companies, so we
recognize where a number of unions bargain with a
single employer that cooperation is the necessary
key to success."

These unions (along with the IUD of the AFL-CIO,
as we shall soon see) had two major goals when
they united: one, to put an end to G. E.'s practice of Boulwarism; and two, to bring more influence to bear on negotiations of new contracts.
Boulwarism, named for Lemuel R. Boulware, a past
vice-president of G. E. for labor relations, was a
paternalistic approach to bargaining. The firm
would analyze those issues relevant to the new
contract and would make one offer. This offer,
they would argue, would be in the best interest of
both the workers and the firm. Usually, such an
offer would not be niggardly by any means. The
problem was that this was not bargaining according
to the NLRB's interpretation of the Taft-Hartley
Act. (G. E. was to be charged more than once with
Unfair Labor Practices over this tactic.) In addition, the offer was traditionally made to the
separate unions, beginning with the weakest and
pattern bargaining thereafter. Given this situation, the unions felt a united front would increase
their bargaining power and allow them to achieve
their goals.

The six unions were initially encouraged by the
IUD to join together. The IUD and George Meany

This case study was drawn entirely from the unpub-
lished dissertation of Abraham Cohen, _Coordinated
Bargaining at General Electric: An Analysis_,
(Cornell University, 1973).

TABLE B.1
The Major Unions at General Electric, 1966

Union (1)	Number of G. E. Locals (2)	Number of G. E. Employees Represented (3)	Total Number of Union Membership (4)
International Union of Electrical, Radio, and Machine Workers (IUE)	65	79,400	270,842
United Electrical, Radio and Machine Workers of America (UE-Independent)	20	16,400	165,000
International Association of Machinists and Aerospace Workers (IAM)	33	12,900	808,065
International Union, United Automobile, Aerospace and Agriculture Implement Workers (UAW)	6	5,700	1,168,067
International Union, Allied Industrial Workers of America (AIW)	2	5,500	69,220
International Brotherhood of Electrical Workers (IBEW)	30	4,500	806,000
Sheet Metal Workers' International Association (SMWIA)	2	3,400	100,000

American Federation of Technical Engineers (AFTE)	9	2,600	15,000
United Steelworkers of America (USWA)	1	945	965,000
International Brotherhood of Teamsters, Chauffeurs, Warehousemen, and Helpers of America (Teamsters-Independent)	3	640	1,506,769
United Association of Journeymen and Apprentices of the Plumbing and Pipe Fitting Industry of the United States and Canada (Plumbers)	3	400	255,765
American Flint Glass Workers' Union of North America (AFGW)	1	150	31,239
Pattern Makers' League of North America	3	90	12,446
International Brotherhood of Firemen and Oilers (IBFO)	3	60	43,000
Total	181	132,685	

himself played active roles in encouraging and
supporting the group that was formed in 1965. In
September, 1965, representatives from the International Union of Electrical, Radio, and Machine
Workers (IUE), by far the largest union at G. E.;
the International Association of Machinists; the
United Automobile Workers; the International
Brotherhood of Electrical Workers; The Allied
Industrial Workers; and the American Federation of
Technical Engineers met with representatives of
the IUD to discuss the upcoming negotiations. In
the following month George Meany met with the
representatives of the unions (now numbering seven
with the addition of the Sheet Metal Workers International Association). At this meeting the Committee on Collective Bargaining (CCB) was formed with
George Meany as Chairman and the presidents of the
seven internationals as members. In March of 1966,
the American Flint Glass Workers joined the group
and brought the total of G. E. employees represented by the CCB to over 90,000.

It was at this time that the CCB informed G. E.
of its desire to have the bargaining structure
altered. The CCB claims it requested coordinated
bargaining and G. E. claims it requested coalition
bargaining. Ultimately, G. E. refused, requesting
that the old bargaining structure remain intact.
One month later the IUE agreed to negotiate separately with G. E. if G. E. would agree to allow
"advisors" from the CCB to sit in on the negotiations. The firm refused and the IUE filed on Unfair Labor Practice with the NLRB. (This Unfair
Labor Practice charge was upheld by the NLRB in
1968 and again on appeal to the U.S. Court of
Appeals in 1969.) In the meantime, G. E. was under
injunction to bargain with the IUE and its advisors. Finally, in September, 1966, G. E. made its
initial offer to the IUE (actually the CCB) and
this was rejected. General Electric was still
holding to its Boulware tactic. A strike seemed
inevitable since the contract deadline was 2 October. All workers represented by the CCB would have
gone on strike at this time, and legally, since
all of their contracts happened to expire at
approximately the same time. However, President
Johnson intervened since G. E. was a producer of
critical material needed for the Vietnam War. He
requested a two week extension of negotiations and
sent in a special negotiating team to avert a

strike. The CCB felt the pressure of a possible Taft-Hartley injunction which they knew would be devastating to their efforts. General Electric had previously argued that coalition/coordinated bargaining would lead to crisis and government intervention, and they proved to be correct in this instance. Under the real threat of an injunction, the CCB decided to accept a compromise agreement (they did most if not all of the compromising) and a strike was averted.

The 1966 negotiations proved unsuccessful to the CCB economically. The final contract agreement was quite similar to G. E.'s initial offer. There were noneconomic benefits though as the CCB did hold together throughout and demonstrated solidarity to its workers and to G. E. This show of unity was to be quite important in setting the stage for the 1969-1970 negotiations.

As was noted earlier, between the 1966 and the 1969-1970 negotiations, the NLRB, upheld by the U.S. Court of Appeals, decided in favor of the IUE in its Unfair Labor Practice charge against G. E. The CCB could be represented at the G. E.-IUE negotiations as long as the negotiations were solely concerned with IUE. When the 1969 session began, the IUD had organized twelve unions that wanted to be part of the negotiating team. Added were the United Steel Workers, the United Association of Journeymen and Apprentices of the Plumbing and Pipe Fitting Industry, the Teamsters, and the International Brotherhood of Firemen and Oilers. This brought the total number of G. E. employees represented to 131,305 (see Table B.2).

The IUD, again led by George Meany, heavily supported this venture. General Electric held to its initial offer in bargaining and the group, now called the Coordinated Bargaining Committee, CBC, rejected this offer. In October, 1969, a strike by the workers of these 12 unions took place; it was to last 100 days. The Federal Mediation and Conciliation Service (FMCS) intervened in November, to no avail, and finally, in January, 1970, Mr. Counts, director of the FMCS, took an active role. General Electric's production had diminished to 10% of capacity and the workers were feeling the pinch of lost income. The public was extremely concerned, especially in the geographic areas hardest hit. (General Electric even convened a conference of 40 concerned mayors in January, 1970.) Finally,

TABLE B.2

Composition of the Coordinated Bargaining Group
at General Electric, 1969

The Unions	Number of Locals at G. E.	Number of Employees Represented
International Union of Electrical, Radio, and Machine Workers (IUE)	71	88,500
International Association of Machinists and Aerospace Workers (IAM)	33	15,500
International Union, United Automobile, Aerospace, and Agricultural Implement Workers (UAW)	5	7,800
International Brotherhood of Electrical Workers (IBEW)	30	5,700
International Union, Allied Industrial Workers of America (AIW)	2	4,800
Sheet Metal Workers' International Association (SMWIA)	2	3,500
American Federation of Technical Engineers (AFTE)	9	2,800
International Association of Teamsters, Chauffeurs, Warehousemen, and Helpers of America (Teamsters)	4	†1,200
United Steelworkers of America (USWA)	1	† 800
United Association of Journeymen and Apprentices of the Plumbing and Pipe Fitting Industry of the United States and Canada	3	† 500
American Flint Glass Workers Union of North America (AFGW)	1	† 150

TABLE B.2 (Continued)

	Number of Locals at G. E.	Number of Employees Represented
International Brotherhood of Firemen and Oilers*	3	55
United Brotherhood of Joiners and Carpenters+	--	--
Federation of Salaried Employees at Westinghouse+	--	--
Total	164	131,305

*The Firemen and Oilers joined the CBC late in 1969.
+The Carpenters and the Federation of Salaried Employees at Westinghouse did not have representative rights at G. E.
†The figures for these unions are somewhat different in other G. E. publications.

at the end of January, both sides compromised and the strike was ended.

When the results of the agreement were made public, it was evident that the CBC had been successful in eliminating the tactic of Boulwarism and bringing more influence to bear on the final outcome. General Electric had made compromises primarily in the areas of wages and cost-of-living adjustments.

Table B.3 gives a summary of all of G. E.'s initial offers and the final settlement. Since compromises by G. E. were made and unity by the CBC maintained, the outcome of the 1969-1970 bargaining session demonstrates the significance of having the bargaining structure changed. This case study adds credence to the arguments that hold bargaining power to be a function of, among other things, bargaining structure. Neil Chamberlin put it best when he observed: "The more employees in the alliance, the greater the cost to their employer of disagreeing on their terms."

TABLE B.3

General Electric's First Offer and the Final Settlement, 1969–1970

Subject	G. E.'s First Offer October 7, 1969	The Final Settlement January 30, 1970
Length of Contract	36 months	40 months
Wage Increase	20¢ an hour—1st year wage reopener—2nd year wage reopener—3rd year	20¢ an hour—immediately 15¢ an hour on 3/1/71 15¢ an hour on 5/1/72
Skilled Trades Adjustment	Additional increases of 5 to 25¢ an hour for high-skill day workers, effective immediately.	Same as in October 7 offer.
Cost-of-Living	No cost-of-living adjustment.	(a) 8¢ maximum per hour each year based on 3 annual adjustments of 1¢ an hour for each 0.3% of Consumer Price Index increase during the preceding year. Effective dates: 10/26/70, 10/71, 10/72. (b) 3¢ of the first year to be paid immediately.
Pensions	Contributory plan with a monthly minimum base ranging from $5 to $7.50 a month per each year of service at age 65, effective 1/1/70.	(a) Same, effective immediately. (b) Minimum base to be increased as follows: 1/1/71-$5.50 to $7.50; 1/1/73-$6.50 to $7.50. (c) 15% increase in past pension credits for long service employees.

Insurance	(a) Several improvements in contributory insurance programs effective at various dates.	(a) Same, plus additional improvements and earlier dates.
	(b) Effective in 2nd year: G. E. to pay employee's insurance plan costs (practically an added 1% pay increase).	(b) Same.
Vacations	(a) 2 weeks after 1 year of service, effective 1/1/71. (b) 4 weeks after 15 years, effective 1/1/72.	Effective 1/1/71: 4 weeks after 15 years; 5 weeks after 30 years.
Sick Pay	Effective 1/1/72: 2 paid days after 5 years 3 paid days after 10 years 4 paid days after 15 years	Effective immediately: Same schedule, plus 5 paid days after 25 years of service.

APPENDIX C

Business Groups' Political Action Committees' Contributions to Presidential Candidates, 1972

Corporation	McGovern	Humphrey	Hartke	Nixon	Schmit
Black and Veatch (Good Govt. Fund)	$	$	$	$ 1,000	$
Cerro Corp. (Cerro Leadership Employees Civic Fund)				19,000	
Consolidated Natural Gas Co. (Consolidated Voluntary Non-partisan Pol. Fund)				500	
Consolidated Natural Gas Service, Inc. (Consolidated Pol. Action Comm.)				1,000	
Eastman Chemical Co. (Volunteers for Better Govt.)				27,000	
Fluor Corp. (Fluor Employees Pol. Fund)				4,000	
General Dynamics Corp. (Effective Citizenship Program)	720.49				
General Electric Co. (Non-partisan Pol. Comm.)	750				
General Telephone Co. of Cal. (Good Govt. Club)				4,000	

Organization				
Gould, Inc. (Better Govt. Assoc.)		1,000	20,000	
Hawaii Telephone Co. (Hawaiian Telephone Employees Good Govt. Club)			2,500	
Hughes Aircraft Co. (Hughes Active Citizenship Fund)	3,807.61	1,015	23,876.65	343
Kerr-McGee Corp. (Kerr-McGee Employees Non-partisan Pol. Comm.)			10,153.75	
Land O'Lakes Cremeries, Inc. (Midwest Pol. Act. Cooperative Trust)		200		
Lockheed Aircraft Corp. (Lockheed Employees Good Citizenship Program)	8,000		50,000	
LTV Aerospace Corp. (Active Citizenship Campaign Fund)			3,108.91	
Medusa Corp. (Medusa Employees Good Govt. Comm.)			160	
Meredith Corp. (Employees Fund for Better Govt.)			2,000	
Minnesota Mining and Manufacturing Co. (Voluntary Pol. Contribution Plan)			1,250	

APPENDIX C (Continued)

Corporation	McGovern	Humphrey	Hartke	Nixon	Schmit
Northrup Corp. (Northrup Good Citizenship Comm.)	1,000			4,180	
Olin Corp. (Olin Executives Voluntary Nonpartisan Pol. Fund)				3,840	
Pacific Lighting Service Corp. (Pacific Lighting Pol. Assist. Comm.)				10,000	
Rex Chainbelt, Inc. (Employees Voluntary Pol. Contribution Plan Comm.)				3,781.02	
Santa Fe Railway Co. (Civic Trust 80)			1,000	6,000 cash[a]	
Sherwin Williams Co. (Comm. for Good Govt.)				125	
Standard Oil (Good Govt. Prog.) Okla., Tex., Inc.				635	
Texas Eastern Trans. Corp. (Employees of)				30,000 cash[a]	

Texas Instruments Co. (Constructive Citizenship Program) Tex., Mass.				21,025
TRW, Inc. (TRW Good Govt. Fund)	5,000			
Union Oil Co. (Political Awareness Fund)				15,500
Union Pacific Railraod (Fund for Effective Govt.)		250		7,860
White, Weld and Co. (White, Weld Nonpartisan Pol. Comm.)				8,000
Youngstown Sheet and Tube Co.				195
Totals	$14,278.10	$7,215	$1,250	$285,690.33 $343

aAmounts from Committee to Re-Elect the President filing, September 28, 1972, under court stipulation in a Common Cause suit.

SOURCE: H. E. Alexander, Financing the 1972 Election, (Lexington, Mass.: Lexington Books, 1976), pp. 698-99.

APPENDIX D

Labor Union Political Action Committee Contributions
to Presidential Candidates, 1972

Union	McGovern	Humphrey	Muskie	Hartke	Mills	Nixon-Agnew
AFL-CIO COPE	$	$	$	$ 4,000	$	$
Amalgamated Clothing Workers	50,746	1,000		250		
Amalgamated Laundry Workers	700					
Amalgamated Meatcutters and Butcher Workmen	56,400	600				
Amalgamated Transit Union	200			250		
American Federation of Musicians		2,000				
American Federation of State, County and Municipal Employees	18,056	600	5,236	250		
American Federation of Teachers	30,536	100				
American Postal Workers Union				125		3,500

Organization				
Brotherhood of Locomotive Engineers		377		
Brotherhood of Railway, Airline and Steamship Clerks, Freight Handlers, Express and Station Employees	5,00	2,500	10,000	10,000
COPE-California		39,500		
COPE-Indiana		200		
COPE-Oregon				200
Communications Workers of America	123,369	8,200	500	
Distributive Workers of America	8,147	135		
Graphic Arts International Union	16,090			
International Assoc. of Machinists and Aerospace Workers-Machinists Non-Partisan Pol. League	113,000	375		
International Brotherhood of Electrical Workers	11,122	110		
International Brotherhood of Painters and Allied Trades		1,000		

APPENDIX D (Continued)

Union	McGovern	Humphrey	Muskie	Hartke	Mills	Nixon-Agnew
International Brotherhood of Teamsters—DRIVE	$ 150	$	$	$	$	$ 19,550
International Chemical Workers Union	1,350					
International Ladies Garment Workers Union	66,792	4,500				
International Union of Automobile Aerospace and Agricultural Implement Workers of America (UAW—Comm. Good Govt. and UAW-V-CAP)	171,176		24,995			
International Union of Electrical Radio and Machine Workers	3,493			250		
International Union of Rubber, Cork, Linoleum and Plastic Workers	16,442	8,140				
Laborers' International Union of N. America						25,000
Marine Engineers Benefic-ial Assoc.-MEBA Pol. Action Fund)		2,000				1,500

National Union of Hospital and Health Care Employees	32,975	2,225			
Operating Engineers					2,000
Retail Clerks International Assoc. Active Ballot Club	74,802	11,926			
Retail Wholesale and Dept. Store Union	1,500				
Seafarers International Union of North America		10,000	1,000	4,000	100,000
Service Employees International		1,000			
Textile Workers Union of America	1,250		250		
Transport Workers of America-Transport Workers Union Pol. Contributions Comm.	15,575	1,000			
United Brotherhood of Carpenters and Joiners of America	3,500	500			
United Furniture Workers of America	2,900				
United Glass and Ceramic Workers of America		365			

APPENDIX D (Continued)

Union	McGovern	Humphrey	Muskie	Hartke	Mills	Nixon–Agnew
United Paperworkers International Union	$	$	$	$	$	$ 3,000
United Steelworkers of America	520	41,699				
United Transportation Union–Transportation Pol. Education League		14,400		3,000		
Miscellaneous Unions	15,319					
Totals	$878,828	$156,952	$30,231	$19,875	$4,000	$164,750

NOTE: Combines data from survey reported in Senate Select Committee on Presidential Campaign Activities, Final Report, No. 93-981, 93rd Cong., 2d sess., June 1974 (Washington, D.C.: U.S. Government Printing Office), pp. 530-33; and from FECA filings recorded in Alphabetical Listing of 1972 Presidential Campaign Receipts, Vols. I and II, Office of Federal Elections, General Accounting Office (Washington, D.C.: U.S. Government Printing Office, November 1973).

SOURCE: H. E. Alexander, Financing the 1972 Election, (Lexington, Mass.: Lexington Books, 1976), pp. 704-6.

APPENDIX E

Leading Corporate PACs in 1976 Elections
(Contributions made in 1975 and 1976)

		Contributions to Federal Candidates
1.	Nonpartisan Political Support Comm. (General Electric Co.)	$109,235
2.	United Technologies Corp. Pol. Action Comm. (United Technologies Corp.)	90,500
3.	Political Awareness Fund (Union Oil Co. of California	86,190
4.	Texaco Employees Pol. Involvement Comm. (Texaco, Inc.)	83,300
5.	Chrysler Nonpartican Pol. Support Comm. (Chrysler Corp.)	71,825
6.	American Family Pol. Action Comm. (American Family Corp.)	71,550
7.	Nonpartisan Comm. for Good Govt. (Coca-Cola Co.)	68,200
8.	Southern Railway Tax Eligible Good Govt. Fund (Southern Railway Co.)	66,830
9.	North Western Officers Trust Account (Chicago Northwestern Transportation)	64,900
10.	Hanson Fund (Tacoma Fund)	62,500

SOURCE: Congressional Quarterly, Inc., Electing Congress (Washington, D.C.: Congressional Quarterly, 1977), p. 27.

APPENDIX F

PACs and Congressional Candidates

	Currently Active Committees	New Committees Since 1/1/75	Contribution to Congressional Candidates 1976
Business, Profession, Agriculture	836	537	$11,562,012
Business	675	485	7,091,374
Health	108	26	2,694,910
Lawyers	8	7	241,280
Agriculture	45	19	1,534,447
Labor	253	92	8,206,578
Miscellaneous	58	26	1,299,928
Ideological	19	3	1,503,394
Total	1,166	658	$22,571,912

SOURCE: Common Cause, Report to the American People on the Financing of Congressional Election Campaigns (Washington, D.C.: Common Cause, May, 1977), p. 7.

Notes

NOTES FOR CHAPTER 1

1. Bonbright and Means, The Holding Company, pp. 55-56.
2. Berle and Means, The Modern Corporation and Private Property, p. 9.
3. Galbraith, The Great Crash, p. 183.
4. Ibid.
5. Ibid., p. 198.
6. See Corwin Edwards, "The Multi-Market Enterprise and Economic Power: Remarks upon Receipt of the Veblen-Commons Award," 285-301; Blair, Economic Concentration; chap. 3, W. Mueller, "Conglomerates: A Non-Industry" in Walter Adams, The Structure of American Industry.
7. Nelson, Merger Movements in American Industry, 1895-1956, p. 37.
8. Scherer, Industrial Market Structure and Economic Performance, p. 105.
9. Josephson, The Robber Barons, chap. 13.
10. Asch, Economic Theory and the Antitrust Dilemma, p. 230.
11. Wilcox and Shepherd, Public Policies Toward Business, p. 204.
12. Asch, p. 238.
13. Asch, p. 240; Scherer, p. 105; Blair, Economic Concentration, pp. 259-60.
14. Asch, p. 231.
15. Scherer, p. 475.
16. Asch, p. 317.
17. Testimony of Stelzer, Hearings on Economic Concentration, pt. 2, p. 182.
18. Ibid.

19. W. Mueller, "The Rising Economic Concentration in America: Reciprocity, Conglomeration and the New Zaibutsu System, p. 16.
20. Ibid.
21. Ibid.
22. An excellent review of the literature is contained in W. Shepherd's The Economics of Industrial Organization, pp. 112-21.
23. Berry, pp. 17-8.
24. Hearings on Economic Concentration, pt. 8A, App. A, pp. 708, 711.
25. "Fortune 500," pp. 240-50.
26. Ibid.
27. Gini coefficients have a range from zero to one, with values closer to zero indicating a more equal distribution and values closer to one indicating a more unequal distribution.
28. Hearings on Economic Concentration, pt. 8A, App. A, p. 706.
29. Fortune Magazine, May and June 1978. These two issues combined contain the "Fortune 1000." A Gini coefficient was generated by using the formula:

$$\text{Gini coefficient} = \frac{.5 - (a+b+c+d+e+f+g+h+i)}{.5}$$

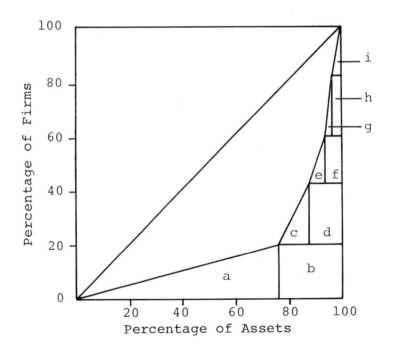

30. Walter Adams, "Conglomerate Granting and Public Policy," p. 249; Narver, p. 105.
31. Edwards, Hearings, pt. 2, p. 42.
32. Cox, Alderson, and Shapiro, pp. 190-212.

NOTES FOR CHAPTER 2

1. For an in depth analysis of the shape of ATC curves, see Goldschmid, Mann, and Weston, chap. 2.
2. Ibid.
3. Ibid.
4. FTC, Economic Report on Conglomerate Mergers, p. 6.
5. Narver, p. 72.
6. Ibid.
7. Bain, Barriers to New Competition, p. 216.
8. Scherer, p. 96.
9. Blair, Economic Concentration, p. 313.
10. Ibid., p. 319.
11. Leibenstein, "Allocative Efficiency vs. X-Efficiency," pp. 392-415.
12. Scherer, p. 405.
13. Leibenstein, pp. 412-13.
14. Scherer, p. 405.
15. Shepherd, p. 378.
16. Leibenstein, pp. 392-415.
17. Jacoby, "The Conglomerate Corporation," pp. 41-53.
18. FTC, Economic Report, p. 97.
19. Merjos, "Takeover Targets: They Share, An Analysis Reveals, A Good Deal in Common," p. 100.
20. Conn, "The Failing Firm/Industry Doctrines in Conglomerate Mergers," p. 187.
21. Dodd and Ruback, "Tender Offers and Stockholder Returns: An Empirical Analysis," pp. 351-73.
22. Conn, p. 100.
23. Weston and Mansinghka, "Tests of the Efficiency Performance of Conglomerate Firms," p. 928.
24. Melicher and Rush, "Evidence of the Acquisitions-Related Performance of Conglomerates," pp. 141-49.
25. Ibid.
26. Three highly publicized hostile merger attempts were American Express' attempt to take over McGraw Hill, Carter-Hawley-Hale's

attempted takeover of Fields Department Stores, and United Technology's successful takeover of Carrier Corporation.
27. "The Biggest Buying Spee Since the 1960's," p. 306.
28. Markowitz, Portfolio Selection: Efficient Diversification of Investments.
29. Scherer, p. 101.
30. Ibid.
31. Lewellen, "A Pure Financial Rationale For the Conglomerate Merger," pp. 521-37.
32. For a thorough discussion of risk, see Malkiel, A Random Walk Down Wall Street, chap. 8.
33. Ibid.
34. Ibid.
35. Ibid.
36. Westerfield, "A Note on the Measurement of Conglomerate Diversification," pp. 909-14.
37. Ibid.
38. Williamson, p. 144.
39. Melicher and Rush, "The Performance of Conglomerate Firms: Recent Risk and Return Experience," pp. 381-88.
40. Ibid.
41. Ibid.
42. Ibid.
43. Ibid.
44. Berle and Means, chap. 6.
45. Cyret and March, Behavioral Theory of the Firm.
46. Baumol, Business Behavior, Value and Growth.
47. Baumol, pp. 46-47. Baumol argues that total revenue is relevant because: (1) consumers will shun a product if they feel the product is falling in popularity; (2) banks are less receptive to firms whose revenues are falling; (3) falling revenues lead to potential loss of distributors; (4) loss of revenue means a loss of market share and therefore a loss of market power; and (5) management salaries are more closely associated with revenues than profit.
48. Baumol, p. 49.
49. Kaysen, in The Corporation in Modern Society, Mason, ed., p. 90.
50. Gordon, Business Leadership in Large Corporations; H. Simon, Administrative Behavior; and Reid, Mergers, Managers and the Economy.
51. McGuire, Chui, and Elbing, "Executive Incomes, Sales and Profits," pp. 753-61.

52. Oliver Williamson, "Managerial Discretion and Business Behavior," pp. 1032-57.
53. Reid.
54. Reid, p. 161.
55. Berle and Means, p. 70.
56. Ibid.
57. Ibid., p. 83.
58. Ibid., p. 56.
59. Edwards, "Conglomerate Bigness As a Source of Power," pp. 331-59.
60. Ibid.
61. Ibid.
62. Donald F. Turner, "Conglomerate Mergers and Section 7 of the Clayton Act," p. 1340.
63. Scherer, chap. 11.
64. Ibid., p. 277.
65. FTC, Economic Report, pp. 432-43.
66. Ibid.
67. O'Hanlon, "August Busch Brews Up a New Spirit in St. Louis," p. 93.
68. Ibid.
69. Ibid., pp. 96-100.
70. FTC, Economic Report, p. 447.
71. Purchasing Magazine, November 20, 1961, pp. 76-77.
72. Hearings on Economic Concentration, pt. 8A.
73. Purchasing Magazine, February 6, 1973, p. 53.
74. Hearings on Economic Concentration, pt. 8A.
75. Ibid., p. 357.
76. Turner, pp. 1391-93.
77. See Steiner, Mergers, pp. 222-23, for a discussion of this case.
78. This example is taken in total from Blair, Economic Concentration, p. 295.
79. Walter J. Mead, "Instantaneous Merger Profit as a Conglomerate Merger Motive," p. 301.
80. Forbes Magazine, January 1, 1970.
81. FTC, Economic Report, pp. 122-24.
82. Ibid.
83. Hearings on Economic Concentration, 91st Cong., pt. 8, 2d sess., pp. 4852-3.
84. Ibid.
85. Hearings, Testimony of A. Briloff, p. 5157.
86. FTC, Economic Report, pp. 152-53.
87. Ibid.

NOTES FOR CHAPTER 3

1.   Edwards, "Conglomerate Bigness as a Source of
     Power," p. 335. Also, a more recent recapitu-
     lation of this argument is made by Edwards in
     "The Multi-Market Enterprise and Economic
     Power: Remarks Upon Receipt of the Veblen-
     Commons Award," pp. 285-301.
2.   Ibid.
3.   Koch, Industrial Organization and Prices,
     p. 148.
4.   Berry, p. 62.
5.   Berry points out his own frustration in not
     being able to obtain current confidential data
     to be used in his analysis.
6.   Peter Steiner has argued that the combination
     of product extension and pure mergers would be
     an acceptable, though not perfect, definition
     of a conglomerate type merger (Mergers, p. 20).
     Berry's analysis led him to use a particular
     number of 2-, 3-, or 4-digit product groups/
     industries as a functional definition (Corpor-
     ate Growth and Diversification, chap. 1-3). He
     coupled this with a Herfindahl index to iden-
     tify the degree of diversification a firm had
     attained. Weston and Mansinghka classified con-
     glomerate (very diversified) firms as those
     involved in more than five 2-digit groups and
     ten 3-digit categories ("Tests of the Effi-
     ciency Performance of Conglomerate Firms,"
     p. 992). Michael Gort argued that a 4-digit
     industry definition was appropriate as long as
     the amount of economic activity within each
     industry was "significant" (Diversification
     and Integration in American Industry, chap. 1).
     Narver, agreeing with Gort, also used a 4-
     digit industry definition when identifying
     conglomerates (very diversified firms). (Con-
     glomerate Mergers and Market Competition.)
7.   The Spearman's Rank Correlation formula is

$$\underline{Y}_{\underline{s}} = 1 - \frac{6 \ \Sigma \ d^2}{\underline{N}^3 - \underline{N}}$$

where

$\underline{d}$ = the difference in ranking of each item and
$\underline{N}$ = the sample size.

NOTES FOR CHAPTER 4

1. Reynolds, p. 351.
2. Ibid., p. 334.
3. Elliott and Cownie, p. 263.
4. Ibid., p. 264.
5. Ibid., p. 263.
6. Hildebrand, pp. 117-18.
7. Ibid.
8. Ibid., p. 124.
9. Hearings on Economic Concentration, pt. 8,
    91st Cong., J. P. Molony, p. 4851.
10. Ibid., p. 4848.
11. Ibid., pp. 4857-58.
12. Kenneth O. Alexander, "Union Structure and
    Bargaining Structure," Labor Law Journal
    (March, 1973):168.
13. Reynolds, p. 444.
14. Hearings, p. 5233.
15. Ibid., p. 4858.
16. Chernish, p. 14.
17. Cohen, "Coordinated Bargaining at General
    Electric: An Analysis," pp. 8-10.
18. Ibid.
19. Taylor and Witney, chaps. 7-9.
20. Ibid., p. 284.
21. Ibid., p. 285.
22. Ibid., p. 734.
23. Ibid., p. 345.
24. Ibid., p. 643.
25. Ibid., p. 382.
26. Wagner, pp. 732-33.
27. Ibid., pp. 733-34.
28. Ibid., p. 735.
29. Alexander, "Union Structure," p. 169.
30. Wagner, pp. 739-40.
31. Ibid.
32. Alexander, "Union Structure," p. 170.
33. Ibid.
34. Farmer, p. 21.
35. Hildebrand, p. 115.
36. Bureau of National Affairs, Labor Relations
    Yearbook, p. 82.
37. Farmer, p. 17.
38. Chernish, p. 29.
39. Farmer, p. 25.
40. Chernish, p. 6.
41. Taylor and Witney, p. 656.
42. Ibid., pp. 658-59.

43. Lahne, "Coalition Bargaining and the Future of
    Union Structure," p. 357.
44. Ibid.

NOTES FOR CHAPTER 5

1. Two associations have recently been formed:
   The Association For Evolutionary Economics and
   The Association For Institutional Thought.
2. Myrdal, "Institutional Economics," p. 774.
3. Klein, "American Institutionalism," p. 258.
4. Berle, p. 3.
5. Ibid., p. 4.
6. Smith, The Wealth of Nations, bk. I, chap. 10.
7. Berle, p. 4.
8. Berle and Means, p. 10.
9. Ibid., p. 13.
10. Ibid.
11. See U. S. Steel vs. U. S.
12. Scherer, p. 114.
13. Bain, p. 102.
14. Landreth, p. 161.
15. See Karl Marx, A Contribution to the Critique
    of Political Economy, pp. 11-12.
16. MacIver, pp. 68-69.
17. Schumpeter, see chap. 14 on Decomposition.
18. Ibid., p. 68.
19. Ibid., chap. 7.
20. Elliot, "Institutionalism as an Approach to
    Political Economy," p. 93.
21. Ibid., p. 94.
22. Ibid.
23. Ibid.
24. Lerner, pp. 438-60.
25. Commons, Institutional Economics; Galbraith,
    The New Industrial State.
26. Commons, p. 7.
27. Alexander, Financing Politics: Money, Elec-
    tions and Political Reform, p. 263. For more
    discussion of this subject see Heard, The
    Costs of Democracy, chap. 5.
28. Edwin Epstein, "Corporations and Labor Unions
    in Electoral Politics," in Herbert Alexander,
    ed., Political Finance: Reform and Reality,
    The Annals of the American Academy of Politi-
    cal and Social Science, 425(May, 1976): 33-58.
    Epstein notes that a PAC is considered to be
    any committee, club, association or other

group of persons that has been registered for
a period of not less than six months, has received contributions from more than 50 persons
and which in aggregate exceed $1000, or has
made expenditures exceeding $1000, and that
makes contributions to five or more candidates
for federal office.

29. Alexander, Financing Politics, p. 264.
30. Epstein, "Corporations and Labor Unions,"
    p. 40.
31. Alexander, Financing Politics, p. 101.
32. Epstein, "Corporations and Labor Unions,"
    p. 53.
33. Ibid.
34. Ibid.
35. Ibid., p. 55.
36. Ibid., p. 50.
37. Alexander, Financing Politics, p. 101.
38. Epstein, "Corporations and Labor Unions,"
    p. 50.
39. Alexander, Financing Politics, p. 126.
40. Ibid., p. 127.
41. Pittman, "Market Structure and Campaign Con-
    tributions," pp. 37-52.
42. Ibid.
43. Ibid.
44. Epstein, The Corporation in American Politics,
    p. 151.
45. Palda, "The Effect of Expenditure on Political
    Success," pp. 745-71.
46. Alexander, Financing Politics, p. 263.
47. Salamon and Siegfried, "The Relationship Be-
    tween Economic Structures and Political Power:
    The Energy Industry," App. H.
48. Ibid. Pittman's statistical tests support this
    as well.
49. National Industrial Conference Board, The Role
    of Business in Public Affairs, Studies in
    Public Affairs, no. 2, (New York, 1968), p. 8.
50. Ibid.
51. Bauer, De Sola Poole, and Dexter, p. 228.
52. Ibid.
53. Ibid., pp. 228-29.
54. Salamon and Siegfried.
55. Business Week, December 20, 1976, pp. 60-63.
56. Gruchy, p. 92.
57. Ayres, The Theory of Economic Progress,
    chap. 10.
58. Ayres, The Industrial Economy, chap. 4.

59. Ibid., p. 186.
60. Ibid., p. 190.
61. N. Jacoby, "The Conglomerate Corporation,"
    p. 45.
62. Galbraith, The New Industrial State.
63. Landreth, p. 358.
64. Galbraith, as reprinted by Elliott and Cownie,
    p. 287.
65. Galbraith, The New Industrial State, p. 392.
66. Epstein, The Corporation in American Politics,
    p. 277.
67. Kornhauser, p. 197.

NOTES FOR CHAPTER 6

1. Narver, p. 120.
2. Narver, pp. 126-30.
3. Narver, p. 130.
4. Donald Turner, "Conglomerate Mergers and Sec-
    tion 7 of the Clayton Act," p. 1363.
5. Berry, p. 160.
6. Steiner, pp. 284-86.
7. Berry, p. 160.
8. Ibid., p. 157.
9. Ibid., pp. 143-44.
10. Williamson, p. 144.
11. Mueller, "Conglomerates: A Non-Industry" in
    W. Adams, The Structure of American Industry,
    5th ed., (New York: Macmillan, 1977), pp. 442-
    81, states their position.
12. Edwards, p. 335.
13. Mueller, "Conglomerates: A Non-Industry,"
    p. 461.
14. Steiner, p. 156.
15. Ibid., p. 159.
16. Asch, see chap. on mergers.
17. Rahl, "Applicability of the Clayton Act to
    Potential Competition."
18. Neal et al., "Report on the White House Task
    Force on Antitrust Policy," p. 33.
19. Ibid., pp. 34-35.
20. Ibid., p. 38.
21. Ibid., pp. 11-13.
22. Ibid.
23. Stigler et al., "Report of the Task Force,"
    p. 31.
24. Reid, "The 'Merger Wage' Phenomenon and Public
    Policy," p. 41.

25. Stigler, "Monopoly and Oligopoly by Merger," pp. 23-30.
26. Ibid., p. 30.
27. Willard Mueller, Antitrust Law and Economic Review, interview with Mueller, Winter, 1969-70, Vol. 3 (no. 2), p. 80.
28. FTC vs. General Foods Corporation.
29. Wilcox and Shepherd, p. 249.
30. Steiner, p. 161.
31. Northwest Industries vs. U. S. The merger did not take place, however, as Northwest was unsuccessful in its effort.
32. Winslow, chap. 13.
33. Ibid.
34. Ibid.
35. Ibid.
36. Ibid. McLaren ordered an independent evaluation of the case to be undertaken by a consultant, Ramsdem. His report, known as the Ramsdem Report, recommended against prosecuting ITT because of the irreparable harm that would come to ITT. Since ITT was expected to bring in about $5 billion over the next 10 years in foreign trade revenue, the harm to ITT would be harm to the U.S. economy. This is an interesting point as it seems being big and diversified can give a firm "special" status when being prosecuted by the Justice Department.
37. Ford Motor Co. and The Electric Autolite Co. vs. U.S.
38. FTC vs. Bendix Corp.
39. Falstaff Brewing Corp. vs. U.S., reversed 410 U.S. 526 (1973).
40. Steiner, p. 277.
41. Fortune Magazine, A. F. Ehrbar, "'Bigness' Becomes the Target of the Trust Busters," May 26, 1979, pp. 34-40.
42. Ibid.
43. Yale Brozen, "The Antitrust Task Force Deconcentration Recommendation," Journal of Law and Economics, 13, (Oct., 1970).
44. Harold Demsetz, "Two Systems of Belief About Monopoly," in Industrial Concentration: The New Learning.
45. Weston and Lustgarten, "Concentration and Wage-Price Charges."
46. Wilcox and Shepherd, p. 5.
47. Peter O. Steiner, Mergers, (Ann Arbor: Univ. of Michigan Press, 1975), p. 334.

Bibliography

BOOKS

Adams, Walter. The Structure of American Industry. New York: Macmillan, 1977.

Adamany, David. Financing Politics. Madison: Univ. of Wisconsin Press, 1969.

___, and Agree, George. Political Money. Baltimore: Johns Hopkins Univ. Press, 1975.

Alexander, Herbert. Financing Politics: Money, Elections and Political Reform. Washington, D.C.: Congressional Quarterly Press, 1976.

___. Financing the 1972 Election. Lexington, Mass.: Lexington Books, 1976.

___. Money in Politics. Washington, D.C.: Public Affairs Press, 1972.

___. Political Finance: Reform and Reality. Philadelphia: The American Academy of Political and Social Science, 1976.

Asch, Peter. Economic Theory and The Antitrust Dilemma. New York: Wiley, 1970.

Ayres, C. The Industrial Economy. Cambridge: Riverside, 1954.

___. The Theory of Economic Progress. Chapel Hill: Univ. of North Carolina Press, 1944.

Bain, Joe S. Barriers to New Competition. Cambridge, Mass.: Harvard Univ. Press, 1956.

___. Industrial Organization. New York: Wiley, 1968.

Bauer, R., De Sola Poole, I., and Dexter, L. American Business and Public Policy. New York: Atherton Press, 1963.

Baumol, W. Business Behavior, Value and Growth. New York: Harcourt, 1967.

Berle, A. A. Economic Power and the Free Society.
    New York: Fund for the Republic, 1957.
Berle, Adolf, and Means, Gardiner. The Modern Cor-
    poration and Private Property. New York: Mac-
    millan, 1940.
Berry, C. Corporate Growth and Diversification.
    Princeton: Princeton Univ. Press, 1975.
Blair, John M. Economic Concentration. New York:
    Harcourt, 1972.
____. The Control of Oil. New York: Pantheon, 1976.
Bonbright, J., and Means, G. The Holding Company.
    New York: Macmillan, 1932.
Chernish, W. N. Coalition Bargaining. Philadelphia:
    Univ. of Pennsylvania Press, 1969.
Clark, J. M. The Control of Trusts. New York:
    Macmillan, 1914.
Cox, Reavis; Alderson, Wroe and Shariro, Stanley.
    Theory in Marketing. Homewood, Ill.: Irwin,
    1964.
Commons, John R. Institutional Economics. New
    York: Macmillan, 1939.
Cyret, R., and March, J. Behavioral Theory of the
    Firm. New York: Prentice Hall, 1963.
Davey, H. Contemporary Collective Bargaining.
    Englewood Cliffs, N.J.: Prentice Hall, 1972.
Dunlop, John T. Industrial Relations Systems.
    Carbondale: Southern Illinois Univ. Press, 1971.
Elliott, John E., and Cownie, John. Competing
    Philosophies in American Political Economics.
    Pacific Palisades: Goodyear, 1975.
Epstein, Edwin. The Corporation in American Poli-
    tics. Englewood Cliffs, N.J.: Prentice Hall,
    1969.
Farmer, Guy. Collective Bargaining in Transition.
    Washington, D.C., Industrial Relations Counse-
    lors, Inc., 1967.
Fortune Plant and Directories, 1965, updated to
    1968.
Galbraith, John K. American Capitalism. Boston:
    Houghton Mifflin, 1952.
____. The Great Crash 1929. Boston: Houghton Mif-
    flin, 1955.
____. The New Industrial State. Boston: Houghton
    Mifflin, 1967.
Goldschmid, H.; Mann, H. M.; and Weston, J. F.
    Industrial Concentration: The New Learning.
    Boston: Little, Brown, 1974.
Gordon, R. Business Leadership in Large Corpora-
    tion. Berkeley: Univ. of California Press, 1961.

Gort, M. Diversification and Integration in Ameri-
     can Industry. Princeton: Princeton Univ. Press,
     1962.
Green, Mark. The Closed Enterprise System. New
     York: Grossman, 1972.
Greer, Douglas. Industrial Organization and Public
     Policy. New York: Macmillan, 1980.
Gruchy, Allen. Contemporary Economic Thought.
     Clifton: Kelly, 1972.
Heard, Alexander. The Costs of Democracy. Chapel
     Hill: Univ. of North Carolina Press, 1960.
Heilbroner, R. The Worldly Philosophers. New York:
     Simon and Schuster, 1953.
Henderson, G. C. The Federal Trade Commission. New
     Haven: Yale Univ. Press, 1924.
Jones, Eliot. The Trust Problem in the United
     States. New York: Macmillan, 1921.
Josephson, Matthew. The Robber Barons. New York:
     Harcourt, 1962.
Kaysen, Carl, and Turner, Donald R. Antitrust
     Policy. Cambridge, Mass.: Harvard Univ. Press,
     1965.
Koch, James. Industrial Organization and Prices.
     Englewood Cliffs, N.J.: Prentice Hall, 1974.
Kornhauser, W. The Politics of Mass Society. New
     York: Free Press, 1959.
Landreth, Harry. History of Economic Theory. Bos-
     ton: Houghton Mifflin, 1976.
Lerner, Max. The Portable Veblen. New York: Viking,
     1965.
Lindblom, Charles. Politics and Markets. New York:
     Basic Books, 1977.
MacIver, R. M. The Web of Government. rev. ed.,
     New York: Free Press, 1965.
Malkiel, B. A Random Walk Down Wall Street. New
     York: Norton, 1975.
Markowitz, Harry. Portfolio Selection: Efficient
     Diversification of Investments. New York:
     Wiley, 1959.
Marx, Karl. A Contribution to the Critique of
     Political Economy. Translated by N. I. Stone.
     Chicago: H. Kerr, 1913.
Mason, Edward, ed. The Corporation in Modern Soci-
     ety. Cambridge, Mass.: Harvard Univ. Press,
     1960.
Mencher, Sam. Poor Law to Poverty Program. Pitts-
     burgh: Univ. of Pittsburgh Press, 1972.
Mintz, M., and Cohen, J. America. New York: Dial
     Press, 1971.

____ and Cohen, J. Power, Inc. New York: Viking
    Press, 1976.
Narver, John C. Conglomerate Mergers and Market
    Competition. Berkeley: Univ. of California
    Press, 1967.
National Industrial Conference Board. The Role of
    Business in Public Affairs. New York: NICB,
    1968.
Nelson, Ralph. Merger Movements in American Indus-
    try, 1895-1956. Princeton: Princeton Univ.
    Press, 1959.
Reid, S. Mergers. Managers and The Economy. New
    York: McGraw-Hill, 1968.
Reynolds, Lloyd. Labor Economics and Labor Rela-
    tions. Englewood Cliffs, N.J.: Prentice Hall,
    1978.
Ripley, William. Trusts, Pools and Corporations.
    Boston: Ginna and Co., 1905.
Scherer, F. M. Industrial Market Structure and
    Economic Performance. Chicago: Rand McNally,
    1970.
Schlesinger, A. The Politics of Upheaval. Boston:
    Houghton Mifflin, 1960.
Schumpeter, Joseph A. Capitalism, Socialism and
    Democracy. New York: Harper, 1975.
Shepherd, William. The Economics of Industrial
    Organization. Englewood Cliffs, N.J.: Prentice
    Hall, 1979.
Simon, H. Administrative Behavior New York: Free
    Press, 1976.
Smith, Adam. The Wealth of Nations. New York: Ran-
    dom House, Modern Library Ed., 1937.
Steiner, Peter. Mergers. Ann Arbor: Univ. of Mich-
    igan Press, 1975.
Taylor, Benjamin, and Witney, Fred. Labor Relations
    Law. Englewood Cliffs, N.J.: Prentice Hall,
    1975.
Veblen, Thorstein. Absentee Ownership. New York:
    B. W. Huebsch, 1923.
____ . Engineers and the Price System. New York:
    Viking, 1921.
____ . Theory of Business Enterprise. New York:
    Scribners, 1937.
Watkins, M. Industrial Combinations and Public
    Policy. Boston: Houghton Mifflin, 1927.
Wilcox, Clair, and Shepherd, William. Public Pol-
    icies Toward Business. Homewood, Ill.: Irwin,
    1975.

Williamson, Oliver. <u>Markets</u> <u>and</u> <u>Hierarchies</u>, <u>Anal-</u>
    <u>ysis</u> <u>and</u> <u>Antitrust</u> <u>Implications</u>. New York: Free
    Press, 1975.
Winslow, John. <u>Conglomerates</u> <u>Unlimited</u>. Blooming-
    ton: Indiana Univ. Press, 1973.

ARTICLES

Alexander, Kenneth O. "Conglomerate Mergers and
    Collective Bargaining." <u>Industrial</u> <u>and</u> <u>Labor</u>
    <u>Relations</u> <u>Review</u> (Apr., 1971): 354-74.
___. "Union Structure and Bargaining Structure,"
    <u>Labor</u> <u>Law</u> <u>Journal</u> (March, 1973): 164-172.
Brozen, Yale. "The Antitrust Task Force Deconcen-
    tration Recommendation." <u>Journal</u> <u>of</u> <u>Law</u> <u>and</u>
    <u>Economics</u> 13 (Oct. 1970): 279-92.
Cohen, Abraham. "Coordinated Bargaining at General
    Electric: An Analysis." Ph.D. dissertation,
    cornell Univ. (1973): 8-10.
Conn, R. "The Failing Firm/Industry Doctrines in
    Conglomerate Mergers." <u>The</u> <u>Journal</u> <u>of</u> <u>Industrial</u>
    <u>Economics</u> (Mar., 1976): 181-187.
Craypo, Charles. "Collective Bargaining in the Con-
    glomerate Multinational Firm: Litton's Shutdown
    of Royal Typewriter." <u>Industrial</u> <u>and</u> <u>Labor</u> <u>Rela-</u>
    <u>tions</u> <u>Review</u> (Oct., 1975): 3-24.
Demsetz, Harold. "Two Systems of Belief About Mono-
    poly." in <u>Industrial</u> <u>Concentration</u>: <u>The</u> <u>New</u>
    <u>Learning</u>: 164-85.
Dodd, Peter, and Ruback, Richard. "Tender Offers
    and Stockholder Returns: An Empirical Analysis."
    <u>Journal</u> <u>of</u> <u>Financial</u> <u>Economics</u> (Dec., 1977):
    351-73.
Edwards, Corwin. "Conglomerate Bigness As A Source
    of Power." in NBER Report <u>Business</u> <u>Concentra-</u>
    <u>tion</u> <u>and</u> <u>Price</u> <u>Policy</u>. Princeton: Princeton
    Univ. Press (1955): 331-59.
Edwards, Corwin. "The Multi-Market Enterprise and
    Economic Power: Remarks upon Receipt of the
    Veblen-Commons Award." <u>Journal</u> <u>of</u> <u>Economic</u>
    <u>Issues</u> (June 1979): 285-301.
"Electing Congress." <u>Congressional</u> <u>Quarterly</u> (Apr.,
    1968): 27.
Elliott, John. "Institutionalism As An Approach To
    Political Economy." <u>Journal</u> <u>of</u> <u>Economic</u> <u>Issues</u>
    Vol. XII, no. 1 (Mar. 1978): 91-114.

Epstein, Edwin. "Corporations and Labor Unions in
    Electorial Politics." in Political Finance:
    Reform and Reality: 33-58.
Hendricks, E. "Conglomerate Mergers and Collective
    Bargaining." Industrial Relations Review (Feb.
    1976): 75-87.
Hildebrand, George. "Cloudy Future For Coalition
    Bargaining." Harvard Business Review (Nov.-Dec.,
    1968): 114-28.
Jacoby, N. "The Conglomerate Corporation." The
    Center Magazine, Vol. 2, no. 4 (July, 1969):
    41-53.
Klein, Phillip. "American Institutionalism."
    Journal of Economic Issues, Vol. 12, no. 2
    (June 1978): 251-76.
Lahne, Herbert. "Coalition Bargaining and the
    Future of Union Structure." Labor Law Journal
    (June, 1967): 353-59.
Leibenstein, Harvey. "Allocative Efficiency vs.
    X-Efficiency." American Economic Review (June,
    1966): 392-415.
Lewellen, Wilbur. "A Pure Financial Rationale For
    The Conglomerate Merger." Journal of Finance
    (Sep., 1970): 521-37.
McGuire, J.; Chiu, J. and Elbing, A. "Executive
    Incomes, Sales and Profits." American Economic
    Review (Sept., 1962): 753-61.
Mead, Walter. "Instantaneous Merger Profit as a
    Conglomerate Merger Motive." Western Economic
    Journal (Dec., 1969): 295-306.
Melicher, R., and Rush, D. "Evidence of the Acqui-
    sitions-Related Performance of Conglomerates."
    Journal of Finance (Mar., 1974): 141-49.
___. "The Performance of Conglomerate Firms:
    Recent Risk and Return Experience." Journal of
    Finance (May, 1973): 381-88.
Mueller, W. "Antitrust and the Market Economy: An
    Interview." Antitrust Law and Economic Review
    (Winter, 1969/70): 37-88.
___. "Conglomerates: A Non-Industry," in Walter
    Adams, The Structure of American Industry:
    442-81.
___. "The Rising Economic Concentration in America:
    Reciprocity, Conglomeration and the New 'Zai-
    butsu' System." Antitrust Law and Economic
    Review, Vol. 4, no. 3 (Spring, 1971): 15-50.
Myrdal, Gunnar. "Institutional Economics." Journal
    of Economic Issues, Vol. 12, no. 2 (Dec., 1978):
    771-84.

Neal, Phil et al. "Report on the White House Task
    Force on Antitrust Policy." as printed in Anti-
    trust Law and Economic Review, Vol. 2, no. 2
    (1968/69): 11-76.
Palda, Kristian. "The Effect of Expenditure on
    Political Success." Journal of Law and Economics
    (Dec., 1975): 745-71.
Pittman, Russell. "Market Structure and Campaign
    Contributions." Public Choice (Fall, 1977): 37-
    52.
Rahl, J. "Applicability of the Clayton Act to
    Potential Competition." Antitrust Law Journal
    143 (1958): 128-45.
Reid, Samuel. "The 'Merger Wave' Phenomena and
    Public Policy." Antitrust Law and Economic
    Review, Vol. 3, no. 1 (Spring, 1969): 25-42.
Salamon, L., and Siegfried. "The Relationship
    Between Economic Structures and Political Power:
    The Energy Industry." contained as Appendix H
    in Competition in the U.S. Energy Industry,
    edited by T. D. Duchesneau. Cambridge: Ballinger,
    1975.
Serot, Julius. "Coalition Bargaining, What Is It?"
    in Coalition Bargaining, Three Views, Proceed-
    ings for the Fourth Annual Labor Management
    Conference, University of Arizona, Jan., 1968.
Stigler, George. "Monopoly and Oligopoly by Mer-
    ger." American Economic Review (May, 1950): 23-
    30.
____ et al. "Report of the Task Force on Productiv-
    ity and Competition." as printed in Antitrust
    Law and Economic Review, Vol. 2, no. 3 (Spring,
    1969): 13-52.
Turner, Donald. "Conglomerate Mergers and Section 7
    of the Clayton Act." Harvard Law Review, Vol.
    78, no. 7 (May, 1965): 1313-95.
Wagner, Lynn E. "Multi-Union Bargaining: A Legal
    Analysis." Labor Law Journal (Dec., 1968): 731-
    42.
Westerfield, Randolph. "A Note on the Measurement
    of Conglomerate Diversification." Journal of
    Finance (Sept., 1970): 904-14.
Weston, J. Fred, and Lustgarten, Steve. "Concen-
    tration and Wage-Price Changes." in Industrial
    Concentration: The New Learning: 307-32.
____ and Mansinghka, S. "Tests of the Efficiency
    Performance of Conglomerate Firms." The Journal
    of Finance (Sept., 1971): 919-36.

Williamson, Oliver. "Managerial Discretion and Business Behavior." American Economic Review, Vol. 53 (1963): 1032-57.

MAGAZINES

"Business's Most Powerful Lobby in Washington," Business Week, Dec. 20, 1976, pp. 60-63.
Ehrbar, A. F. "Bigness Becomes the Target of the Trust Busters," Fortune, Mar. 26, 1979, pp. 34-42.
___. "Corporate Takeovers Are Here to Stay." Fortune, May 8, 1978, pp. 90-102.
Forbes, Jan. 1, 1970, pp. 96-98.
"Fortune 500," Fortune, May, 1978, pp. 238-59.
"Fortune Second 500," Fortune, June, 1978, pp. 170-91.
Merjos, Anna. "Takeover Targets: They Share, An Analysis Reveals, A Good Deal in Common." Barrons, May, 1978, p. 100.
O'Hanlon, Thomas. "August Busch Brews Up a New Spirit in St. Louis," Fortune, Jan. 15, 1979, pp. 92-103.
Purchasing Magazine, Feb. 6, 1973, p. 53.
Purchasing Magazine, Nov., 1961, pp. 76-77.
"The Biggest Buying Spree Since the 1960's," Fortune, May 7, 1979, p. 306.

GOVERNMENT DOCUMENTS

Adams, Walter. "Conglomerate Giantism and Public Policy." Statement Before the U.S. Senate Antitrust and Monopoly Subcommittee, July 27, 1978.
Congressional Quarterly. Washington, D.C., Apr. 1978; June, 1973.
Federal Trade Commission. Statistical Report on Mergers and Acquisitions. Washington, D.C., 1977.
Hearings on Economic Concentration. pts. 1, 2, 8, 8A, 88th, 89th and 91st Congresses.

OTHER

Annual Reports on 10-K of the 200 largest manufacturing firms filed with the SEC, 1977.
Bureau of National Affairs, Labor Relations Yearbook. 1967.

CASES

AFL-CIO Joint Negotiating Committee for Phelphs
    Dodge vs. NLRB, 184 NLRB 976.
American Radiator and Standard Sanitary Corp. vs.
    NLRB, 155 NLRB 736 (1965).
Bendix Corp., vs. FTC, 450 F. 2d 534 (6th Cir.
    1971).
Borg-Warner vs. NLRB, 356 U.S. 342 (1958).
Buckley vs. Valco, 44 USLW 412 (1976).
Columbia Steel vs. U.S., 334 U.S. 495, 1948.
El Paso Natural Gas vs. U.S., 376 U.S. 651 (1964).
Falstaff Brewing Co. vs. U.S., 332 F. Supp. 970
    (D. R.I., 1971).
Ford Motor Co. and The Electric Autolite Co. vs.
    U.S., 286, F. Supp. 407, (E.D. Mich., 1968),
    315 F. Supp. 372 (E.D. Mich., 1970), and in a
    Supreme Court Review, U.S. vs. Ford Motor Co.,
    405 U.S. 526 (1972).
General Dynamics vs. U.S., 258 F. Supp. 36
    (S.D.N.Y.), 1966.
General Electric vs. NLRB, 418 F. (2d) 736 (1969).
General Foods vs. FTC, 386 F. 2d 936 (3d Cir.);
    391 U.S. 919, 1967.
ITT (Canteen) vs. U.S., 1971 CCH Trade Cases
    73,619 (N.D. ILL. 1971).
ITT (Grinnell) vs. U.S., 306 F. Supp. 766 (D.
    Conn.) 1969.
ITT (Hartford) vs. U.S., 306 F. Supp. 766 (D.
    Conn.) 1969.
Ling-Temco-Vought vs. U.S., 315 F. Supp. 1301
    (W.D. Pa.) 1970.
Northern Securities vs. U.S., 193 U.S. 197 (1904).
Northwest Industries vs. U.S., 301 F. Supp. 1066
    (N.D. Ill. 1969).
Proctor and Gamble vs. FTC, 386 U.S. 568 (1967).
Standard Oil of New Jersey vs. U.S., 221 U.S. 1
    (1911).
U.S. Pipe and Foundry, 298, F. 2d 873, 44 17,412,
    1962.
U.S. Steel vs. U.S., Rule of Reason Decision, 223
    F. 55 (1915).

Index

Wagner Act. <u>See</u> National Labor Relations Act
Workers, rights of, 84-85

X-efficiency, 19-20
X-inefficiency, 18-19

AUTHORS

Alexander, Herbert, 103, 105, 106
Alexander, Kenneth O., 74, 82
Ayres, Clarence, 108-9

Bauer, Raymond, 107
Baumol, William, 27
Berle, Adolph A., 2, 26, 29
Berry, Charles, 9, 61, 120
Boulware, Lemuel, 141
Brigham, Eugene, 40
Briloff, Abraham, 42
Brozen, Yale, 132, 133
Brubaker, Mr. (testimony of), 73-74

Chiu, John S., 27
Cohen, Abraham, 141
Commons, John R., 102
Conn, Robert L., 21
Craypo, Charles, 139
Cyert, Richard M., 26

Darwin, Charles, 88, 89
Demsetz, Harold, 132-33
de Sola Poole, Ithiel, 107
Dexter, Lewis, 107
Dodd, Peter, 21

Edwards, Corwin, 12, 30, 44, 122
Elbing, Alvar, 27
Epstein, Edwin, 106, 113

Farmer, Guy, 84

Galbraith, John K., 3, 72, 101, 110-14
Gordon, Robert, 27

Jefferson, Thomas, 91
Johnson, President Lyndon, 126

Charles R. Spruill is Assistant Professor of Economics at Appalachian State University. His research and writing have been concentrated within the topics of industrial organization, collective bargaining, and political economy. This book developed from his perception that the traditional atomistic view of market competition is giving way to competition among large, multiproduct, corporate firms that have much in common by way of goals, problems, and methods of solution.